SHOW WHAT YOU

WASL

FOR GRADE 3

grade
3

PREPARATION FOR THE
WASHINGTON ASSESSMENT
OF STUDENT LEARNING

Show What You Know®
Publishing

NAME

Published by:
Show What You Know® Publishing
A Division of Englefield & Associates, Inc.
P.O. Box 341348
Columbus, OH 43234-1348
Phone: 614-764-1211
www.showwhatyouknowpublishing.com
www.passthewasl.com

WASL Item Distribution information was obtained from the Washington Office of Superintendent of Public Instruction website, March 2006.

Printed in the United States of America
08 07 06   20 19 18 17 16 15 14 13 12 11 10 9 8 7 6 5 4 3 2

ISBN: 1-59230-183-5

Acknowledgements

Show What You Know® Publishing acknowledges the following for their efforts in making this assessment material available for Washington students, parents, and teachers.

Cindi Englefield, President/Publisher
Eloise Boehm-Sasala, Vice President/Managing Editor
Christine Filippetti, Project Editor
Jill Borish, Project Editor
Charles V. Jackson, Project Editor
Jennifer Harney, Illustrator

About the Contributors

The content of this book was written BY teachers FOR teachers and students and was designed specifically for the Washington Assessment of Student Learning (WASL) for Grade 3. Contributions to the Reading and Mathematics sections of this book were also made by the educational publishing staff at Show What You Know® Publishing. Dr. Jolie S. Brams, a clinical child and family psychologist, is the contributing author of the Worry Less About Tests and Test-Taking Hints for Test Heroes chapters of this book. Without the contributions of these people, this book would not be possible.

Introduction

Dear Student:

This *Show What You Know® on the WASL for Grade 3, Student Workbook* was created to give you practice for the Washington Assessment of Student Learning (WASL) in Reading and Mathematics.

The first two chapters in this workbook—Worry Less About Tests and Test-Taking Hints for Test Heroes—were written just for third-grade students. Worry Less About Tests offers advice on how to overcome nervous feelings you may have about tests. The Test-Taking Hints for Test Heroes chapter includes helpful tips on how to answer questions correctly so you can succeed on the WASL.

The next two chapters of this Student Workbook will help you prepare for the Reading and Mathematics WASL.

- The Reading chapter includes a Reading Practice Tutorial, two full-length Reading Assessments (Reading Assessment One—Session One and Session Two, Reading Assessment Two—Session One and Session Two), and a Glossary of Reading Terms that will help you show what you know on the WASL.
- The Mathematics chapter includes a Mathematics Practice Tutorial, a full-length Mathematics Assessment (Session One, Session Two, and Session Three), a Glossary of Mathematics Terms, and a Glossary of Mathematics Illustrations that will help you show what you know on the WASL.

This Student Workbook will help you become familiar with the look and feel of the WASL and will provide a chance to practice your test-taking skills so you can show what you know.

Good luck on the WASL!

 © Englefield & Associates, Inc.

Table of Contents

This page intentionally left blank.

Worry Less About Tests

Introduction

Many of us get nervous or anxious before taking a test. We want to do our best, and we worry that we might fail. You may have heard of the Washington Assessment of Student Learning (WASL), although you may not be familiar with the actual WASL assessment. Because the WASL is new to you, you may become scared. You may worry about the test, and this might interfere with your ability to show what you know.

This chapter offers tips you can use on the WASL and many other tests. The ideas will build your test-taking confidence.

Worry Less About Tests

There are many things most of us would rather do than take a test. What would you rather do? Go to recess? See a movie? Eat a snack? Go swimming? Take a test? Most of us would not choose take a test. This doesn't mean we're afraid of tests. It means we like to do things that are more fun!

Some students do not want to take tests for another reason. They are afraid of tests and are afraid of failing. Even though they are smart enough to do well, they are scared. All of us worry about a test at one time or another. So, if you worry about tests, you are not alone.

When people worry about tests or are scared of tests, they have what is called test stress. You may have heard your parents say, "I'm feeling really stressed today." That means they have worried feelings. These feelings of stress can get in the way of doing your best. When you have test stress, it will be harder to show what you know. This chapter will help you get over your stress and worry less. You won't be scared. You will feel calm, happy, and proud.

If your mind is a mess
Because of terrible stress,
And you feel that you can't change at all.
Just pick up this book,
And take a look,
Our tips won't let you fall!

It's OK to Worry a Little Bit

Most people worry a little bit about something. Worrying isn't always a bad thing. A small amount of worrying is helpful. If you worry about crossing the street, you are more careful. When you worry about your school work, you work hard to do it right. As you can see, a little worrying isn't bad. However, you have to make sure you don't let worrying get in the way of doing your best. Think about crossing the street. If you worry too much, you'll never go anywhere. You can see how worrying too much is not a good thing.

Third graders have a very special job. That job is taking the WASL. The people who give the WASL want to know what you're learning in school. WASL stands for Washington Assessment of Student Learning. All children in Washington are terrific and can learn to do their best on the WASL without worrying too much or too little.

What Kind of Kid Are You?

Test stress and worrying too much or too little can get in your way. The good news is there are ways you can help yourself do better on tests. All you have to do is change the way you think about taking tests. You can do better, not just by learning more or studying more, but by changing the way you think about things.

Now you will read about some students who changed the way they think about tests. You may see that these students have some of the same feelings you have. You will learn how each of these kids faced a problem and ended up doing better on tests.

Stay-Away Stephanie

Stephanie thought that it was better to stay away from tests than to try at all. She was scared to face tests. She thought, "If I stay home sick, I won't have to take the test. I don't care if I get in trouble; I'm just not going to take the test." Stay-Away Stephanie felt less nervous when she ran away from tests, but she never learned to face her fear. Stephanie's teacher thought Stephanie didn't care about tests or school, but this wasn't true at all. Stay-Away Stephanie really worried about tests. She stayed away instead of trying to face each challenge.

One day, Stephanie's mom had an idea! "Stephanie, do you remember when you were afraid to ride your bike after I took the training wheels off?" her mom said. "You would hide whenever I wanted to take a bike ride. You said, 'I would rather walk than learn to ride a two-wheel bike.'" Stephanie knew that wasn't true. She wanted to learn to ride her bike, but she was scared. She stayed away from the challenge. When Stephanie faced her fear, step by step, she learned to ride her bike. "Stephanie," her mom said, "I think you stay away from tests because you're worried." Stephanie knew her mom was right. She had to face tests step by step.

Stephanie and her teacher came up with a plan. First, Stephanie's teacher gave her two test questions to do in school. For homework, Stephanie did two more questions. When Stephanie was scared, she talked with her mom or her teacher. She didn't stay away. Soon, Stephanie knew how to ask for help, and she took tests without being worried. Now, she has a new nickname: Super-Successful Stephanie!

If you are like Stay-Away Stephanie, talk with your teacher or someone who can help you. Together, you can learn to take tests one step at a time. You will be a successful student instead of a stay-away student.

Worried Wendy

Wendy always thought that the worst would happen. Her mind worried about everything. "What if I can't answer all the questions? What if I don't do well? My teacher won't like me. My dad will be upset. I will have to study a lot more." Wendy spent her time worrying. Instead, she should have learned to do well on tests.

Wendy was so worried her stomach hurt. Wendy's doctor knew she wasn't sick; she was worried. "Wendy," he said, "I have known you ever since you were born. You have always been curious. You wanted to know how everything worked and where everything was. But now your curious mind is playing tricks on you. You are so worried, you're making yourself sick."

Wendy's doctor put a clock on his desk. "Look at this clock. Is it a good clock or a bad clock?" Wendy had no answer. "Believe it or not, Wendy, we can trick our minds into thinking it is good or bad. I'm going to say bad things about this clock as fast as I can. First, it's not very big. Also, because the clock is small, I might not read the time on it correctly. Since the clock is so small, I might lose it forever." Wendy agreed it was a bad clock. "But wait," said her doctor. "I think the clock is a neat shape, and I like the colors. I like having it in my office; it tells time well. It didn't cost much, so if I lose it, it isn't a big deal." Wendy realized she could look at tests the way the doctor looked at the clock. You don't have to worry. You can see good things, not bad.

Critical Carlos

Carlos always put himself down. He thought he failed at everything he did. If he got a B+ on his homework, he would say, "I made so many mistakes, I didn't get an A." He never said good things like, "I worked hard. I'm proud of my B+." Carlos didn't do well on tests because he told himself, "I don't do well on anything, especially tests."

Last week, Carlos got a 95% on a test about lakes and rivers. Carlos stared at his paper. He was upset. "What is the matter, Carlos?" his teacher asked. "Is something wrong?" Carlos replied, "I'm stupid; I missed five points. I should have gotten a 100%."

"Carlos, nobody's perfect: not me, not you, not anybody. I think 95 out of 100 is super! It's not perfect, but it is very good. Celebrate, Carlos!" Carlos smiled; he knew his teacher was right. Now, Carlos knows he has to feel good about what he does. He isn't sad about his mistakes. He's cheerful, not critical.

Look at the chart below. Use this chart to find out all the good things about yourself. Some examples are given to get you started.

Good Things About Me
1. *I make my grandmother happy when I tell her a joke.*
2. *I taught my dog how to shake hands.*
3. *I can do two somersaults in a row.*
4.
5.
6.

Victim Vince

Vince couldn't take responsibility for himself. He said everything was someone else's fault. "The WASL is too hard. I won't do well because they made the test too hard. And, last night, my little brother made so much noise that I couldn't write my homework story. It's his fault I won't do well. I asked Mom to buy my favorite snack. I have to have it when I study. She forgot to pick it up at the store. I can't study without my snack. It's her fault." Vince complained and complained.

Vince's aunt told him he had to stop blaming everyone for his troubles. "You can make a difference, Vince," she said. "When is your next test?" Vince told her he had a spelling test on Friday. "You're going to be the boss of the test. First, let's pick a time to study. How is every day at 4:00 p.m.?" Vince agreed. "Now, how are you going to study?"

"I like to practice writing the words a couple of times," Vince said. "Then, I ask Mom or Dad to quiz me."

"Great idea. Every day at 4:00 p.m., you're going to write each word four times. Then, ask one of your parents to review your list. You're the boss of the spelling test, Vince, because you have a plan."

Vince's Study Plan

TIME	Monday	Tuesday	Wednesday	Thursday	Friday
					Spelling Test!
4:00	Write down spelling words. Then, ask Mom or Dad to help.	Write down spelling words. Then, ask Mom or Dad to help.	Write down spelling words. Then, ask Mom or Dad to help.	Write down spelling words. Then, ask Mom or Dad to help.	
4:30					
5:00					
5:30					
6:00					
7:00	Look at spelling words again.	Look at spelling words again.	Look at spelling words again.	Look at spelling words again.	
7:30					Get a movie for doing well!

When Friday came, Vince's whole world changed. Instead of being in a bad mood because of a poor grade, Vince felt powerful! He took his spelling test and scored an A-. Vince could not believe his eyes! His teacher was thrilled. Vince soon learned he could control his attitude. Vince is no longer a victim. Instead, he is Victor Vince.

Perfect Pat

Pat spent all her time studying. She told herself, "I **should** study more. I **should** write this book report over. I **should** study every minute for the WASL." Trying hard is fine, but Pat worked so much, she never felt she had done enough. Pat always thought she should be studying. Pat would play with her friends, but she never had a good time. In the middle of kickball or crafts, Pat thought, "I should be preparing for the WASL. I should be writing my book report." When Pat took a test, she worried about each question. "I can't answer this one. I should have studied harder."

"Pat," her principal said, "you have to relax. You're not enjoying school." Pat replied, "I can't do that. There is so much more to learn." The principal gave Pat some tips on how to use her study time better.

- Do not study for long periods of time. Instead, try to work for about 10–20 minutes at a time, and then take a break. Everyone needs a break!

- Ask yourself questions as you go along. After you study a fact, test yourself to see if you remember it. As you read, ask yourself questions about what you are reading. Think about what you are studying!

- Find a special time to study. You may want to think of a good time to study with the help of your parents or your teacher. You could choose to study from 4:30 to 5:00 every day after school. After dinner, you could work from 7:30 to 8:00. After you finish studying, do not worry! You have done a lot for a third grader.

- Remember, you are a third-grade kid! School is very important, but playing, having fun, and being with your friends and family are also very important parts of growing up. Having fun does not mean you won't do well in school. It doesn't mean you will do poorly on the WASL either. Having fun in your life makes you a happier person and helps you do better on tests.

"Everyone Else Is Better" Edward

Edward worried about everyone else. During holidays, Edward thought about the presents other people received. At his baseball game, he worried his teammates would score more runs. Edward always wanted to know how his friends did on tests. He spent so much time worrying about what other people were doing, he forgot to pay attention to his own studying and test taking.

"Edward, you're not going to succeed if you don't worry about yourself," his grandfather told him. "You need to start talking about what **you** can do. Instead of asking your friend how he did on a test, you say, 'I got an 85%. Next time, I want to get a 90%.'" When Edward practiced this, he worried less about tests and was a whole lot happier.

Shaky Sam

Sam was great at sports. He was friendly and funny, and he had many friends. However, Sam had one big problem. Every time he thought about taking a test, he would start shaking inside. His heart would start pounding like a drum. His stomach would get upset. Even the night before a test, he started shaking really hard.

Sam's older brother liked to sing. He told Sam he used to get nervous before he sang to a crowd of people. "Sam, you need to trick your body. Don't think about the test; think about something fun and happy."

Sam closed his eyes. He thought about making four shots in a row on the basketball court. He thought about his favorite dessert: vanilla ice cream. He thought about swimming in his neighbor's pool. When he opened his eyes, he wasn't shaking.

Practice thinking happy thoughts, and make believe you are far away from your troubles. Test stress will disappear.

Other Ways That Third Graders Have Stopped Worrying About Tests

Third graders are pretty smart kids. They have lots of good ideas for getting rid of test stress. Here are some ideas from other third graders.

- When I am scared or worried, I talk to my neighbor. She is 70 years old. She is the smartest person I know. We sit on her porch and eat cookies and talk. It makes me feel better to know that she had some of the same problems when she was in third grade. She did well in school, and I know I can, too.

- Everything is harder in third grade, especially reading and math. I didn't want to go to school. I talked to my teacher, and he said we should have a talk every day before class. We talk about my homework, and he gives me tips. This really calms me down. When I am calm, I always do better.

- I used to worry that I wasn't doing well in school. I thought everyone else was smarter. My dad gave me a special folder. I keep all my tests in it. When I look at the tests, I see how much I have learned. I know I am doing a good job.

Washington kids are smart kids! You, your teachers, and your family and friends can help you find other ways to beat test stress. You will be surprised how much you know and how well you will do on the WASL.

Test-Taking Hints for Test Heroes

Introduction

Many third graders have not seen a test like the WASL on which they have to fill in answer bubbles or write answers on lines. Before you sit down to take a test, it is a good idea to review problem-solving and test-taking hints.

This chapter offers many hints you can use when you take the WASL and other tests. The ideas will build your confidence and improve your test-taking skills.

Do Your Best on the WASL: Think Like a Genius!

Most third graders think the smartest kids do the best on tests. Smart kids may do well on tests, but all kids can do their best. By learning some helpful hints, most kids can do better than they ever thought they could on tests.

Learning to do well on tests will be helpful to you throughout your whole life, not just in third grade. Kids who are test smart feel very good about themselves. They have an "I can do it" feeling about themselves. This feeling helps them succeed in school, in sports, and in music. It even helps with making friends. Test-smart kids usually do well in their school work, too. They believe they can do anything.

Become an Awesome Test Hero!

1. Fill In the Answer Bubble

You will use a pencil to take the WASL. Think about tests you have taken. To answer questions, you may have written an answer, circled the correct answer, or solved a math problem. The WASL is different. You will use your pencil to fill in answer bubbles. The test is mostly multiple choice, but there are a few short-answer and extended-response questions for which you will write your answers on lines.

For each multiple-choice question, you will have three choices to pick from. After you read the question and all the answer choices, think about which choice is correct. Next to each choice, you will see an answer bubble. The answer bubbles are not very big. They are smaller than the end of an eraser, smaller than a dime, and smaller than a jellybean. Even though the answer bubbles are small, they are very important. To answer each question, you must fill in the answer bubble next to the correct choice. Only fill in one answer bubble for each multiple-choice question. Fill in the bubble all the way, and do not color outside the bubble. Make sure you fill in the answer bubble neatly when you take the WASL.

Look at the example below. You can see the correct way to fill in an answer bubble. Practice filling in the answer bubbles in this example.

There was a girl named Devine,
Who thought that a dot was a line!
She didn't fill in the bubble;
She was really in trouble!
When her answers are wrong she will whine!

Correct: ● Incorrect: ●

Practice filling in the answer bubbles here: ○   ○   ○   ○   ○   ○

Learning how to fill in answer bubbles takes practice, practice, and more practice! It may not be how you are used to marking the correct answer, but it is one way to give a right answer on the WASL. Think about Kay!

A stubborn girl named Kay,
Liked to answer questions her own way.
So her marked answer bubbles,
Gave her all sorts of troubles.
Her test scores ruined her day!

You will also have to answer short-answer and extended-response questions. These are questions for which you have to write the answer. Some questions will only require one or two words or short phrases, but other questions may require a full sentence or two. Remember to write clearly and neatly so that people can read what you have written. Correct spelling and proper grammar will help to make your response clear. However, if you misspell a word or forget to use a comma or period, it will not be counted against you. The most important thing to remember when you answer short-answer and extended-response questions is to completely answer the question as best you can.

2. Only Fill In the Answer Bubbles You Need To

It is not a good idea to touch the answer bubbles with your pencil until you are ready to fill in the right answer. If you put marks on more than one answer bubble, the computer that grades your test won't know which choice you think is right. Sometimes, kids get a little worried during the test. They might play with their pencils and tap their answer booklets. This is not a good idea. Look at all the answer choices. Only fill in one answer bubble for each multiple-choice question. This should be the answer bubble for the choice you think is right. Do not put marks in any other answer bubbles.

There was a nice girl named Sue,
Who thought she knew what to do.
She marked all the spots.
Her paper was covered with dots!
And she didn't show all that she knew.

© Englefield & Associates, Inc.

3. Think Good Thoughts

The better you feel about taking tests, the better you will do. Imagine you are a famous sports hero. You feel good about playing your favorite sport. You feel good about yourself. As a sports hero, you don't start a soccer game, football game, baseball game, tennis match, or swimming meet by saying, "This is going to be hard. I can't do it." Instead you say, "This may be a little hard, but I can do it. I am glad I have a chance to do this. I am going to do my best. I know I can." You may think the WASL is a little hard, but you can do it. When you start the WASL, remember to think good thoughts. This will help you to be the best test hero you can be.

There was a girl named Gail,
Who thought she always would fail.
She said, "Tests are tough,
I'm not smart enough."
She had a sad end to her tale.

4. What Happens if I Don't Do Well on the Test?

The WASL is one way to find out how much you have learned by the third grade. It is important to try your best on the WASL, but remember, your friends, parents, and teachers will like you no matter how you do on this test.

There was a nice boy named Chad,
Who thought if he failed he was bad.
His teacher said, "That's not true.
I like you no matter how you do."
Now Chad is glad and not sad

5. Don't Be Too Scared or Too Calm

Being too scared about tests will get in the way of doing your best. If you are scared, you won't be able to think clearly. If you are scared, your mind can't focus on the test. You think about other things. Your body might start to feel nervous. There is a chapter in this book called "Worry Less About Tests." It will help you feel calmer about tests. Read that chapter so you can feel calmer about the WASL and other tests.

If you are too calm before taking a test, you might not do well. Sometimes, kids say, "I don't care about this!" They might not have pride in their school work. They may be nervous. They may think the WASL is "no big deal" and may try to forget about it. If you do not think a test is important and you try to forget about it, you are not thinking good thoughts. Don't be scared of the test, but don't forget about it. You can become a test hero and do your best if you take pride in your work.

There was a student named Claire,
Who usually said, "I don't care."
Her sister named Bess,
Always felt total stress.
They weren't a successful pair!

6. Don't Rush; Speeding Through the Test Doesn't Help

The last time you took a test, did you look around the room to see who finished first? If someone handed his or her paper in before you, did you feel like you needed to hurry up? Kids feel that way sometimes, but rushing through questions will not help you on the WASL. Finishing the WASL first, or second, or even third is not important. This may be a surprise to learn. Usually, we think speed is good. We hear about the fastest computer, the fastest runner, and the fastest car. Speed is exciting to think about, but working fast on the WASL will not make your test score better. Take your time, and you will be able to show what you know!

There was a third grader named Liz,
Who sped through her test like a whiz.
She thought she should race
At a very fast pace,
But it caused her to mess up her quiz.

7. Read Directions Carefully!

One of the best ways to become a test hero is to read directions. Directions help you understand what you're supposed to do. On the WASL, it is really important to take your time and to read directions. You may say, "Why should I read directions? I know what to do." Here's a story that may change your mind.

Imagine you are a famous baker. Everyone thinks you make the best cakes in Washington! One day, a group of kings and queens comes to Washington for an important visit. They ask you to bake a special cake for them. You have never baked this type of cake before. The kings and queens give you directions, but you don't read them. You think to yourself, "Who has time? I don't need directions. I know how to bake cakes." You don't read the directions but put them in a drawer. This is not a good idea. The directions tell you to bake the special cake at 250 degrees, but you bake the cake at 350 degrees! What do you get? A very crispy cake and very angry kings and queens. You should have read the directions!

Make sure you read directions slowly and repeat them to yourself. You should understand the directions before you begin the test.

There was a nice boy named Fred,
Who ignored almost all that he read.
The directions were easy,
But he said, "I don't need these!"
He should have read them instead.

8. Don't Get Stuck on One Question

Some of the questions on the WASL will be easy. Other questions might be a little harder. Don't let that worry you! If there is a question you're not sure how to answer, use your pencil to put a mark by the question. Remember, mark the question, not the answer choice bubbles. Once you have marked the hard question, move on to the next question. When you get to the end of the test, go back and try to answer the hard question. Once you have answered many easy questions, you might be able to answer the hard question with no problem.

If you circle a question and move on, you won't get stuck. This is a good hint. The WASL has lots of questions, so you will be able to show what you know. If there is a question that puzzles your mind, just go back to it later.

There was a sweet girl named Von,
Who got stuck and just couldn't go on.
She'd sit there and stare,
But the answer wasn't there.
Before she knew it, all the time was gone.

9. Use What You Know!

By the time you take the WASL, you will have been in school for four years. You went to kindergarten, first grade, and second grade, and now you are in the third grade. You were taught lots of things in school, but you learned many things in other places, too. You may have gathered information at the library, in a magazine, from TV, from your parents, and from lots of other places. Third graders have a lot of information in their brains!

Sometimes, third graders forget how much they know. You may see a question that your teacher has not talked about. This is OK. You may have heard about it somewhere else. Take a minute to think about all you know.

Let's say you were asked the following question.

Melissa and her family go to Florida for a vacation. Melissa is excited about going to the beach and to an amusement park. She also really enjoys fresh orange juice. Melissa wants to walk to a store to buy an orange juice treat. The sign says the store is 200 yards away. If Melissa walks to the store, about how long will it take her?

○ A. About 5 minutes

○ B. About 30 minutes

○ C. About 1 hour

This seems like a hard question. You don't know how far 200 yards is. Stop and think for minute! You have heard the word "yard" before, but where? You may have heard it used in a football game; a football field is 100 yards. So 200 yards is about the length of two football fields. You know it will not take long to walk that far. Now you know the right answer; it will probably only take about 5 minutes. Even though you thought you didn't know the answer, you used the information you remembered from other places. You're on your way to becoming a test hero!

There was a boy named Drew,
Who forgot to use what he knew.
He had lots of knowledge.
He could have been in college,
But his correct answers were very few.

10. Luck Isn't Enough!

Have you ever had a lucky number, a lucky color, or even a lucky hat? Everyone believes in luck. A famous football player always wears the same shoes game after game because he thinks they give him good luck. This doesn't make any sense. Wearing old, smelly shoes doesn't help him play well. But he believes in luck anyway. Believing in luck can be fun, but it is not going to help you do well on the WASL. The best way to do well is to PRACTICE! Listening to your teacher, practicing the hints you have learned in this book, and learning every day in the third grade will help you do your best.

There was a cool boy named Chuck,
Who thought taking tests was just luck.
He never prepared.
He said, "I'm not scared."
When his test scores appear, he should duck!

11. Recheck Your Answers

Everyone makes mistakes. Checking your work is very important. There once was a famous magician. He was very good at what he did, but he never checked his work. One night, he was getting ready for a big magic show. There were hundreds of people watching the show. The magician's wife said, "Check your pockets for everything you need." The magician didn't listen. "I've done this a million times," he said to himself. "I don't need to check my pockets." What a bad idea! When he got on stage, he reached his hand into an empty pocket—no magic tricks! Next time, he will recheck his pockets to do the best job possible!

Going back and checking your work is very important. You can read a paragraph over again if there is something that you do not understand or something you forget. You will not be wasting time if you recheck your work. It is important to show what you know, not to show how fast you can go. Making sure you have put down the right answer is a good idea.

There was a quick girl named Jen,
Who read stuff once and never again.
It would have been nice
If she'd reread it twice.
Her scores would have been better then!

Helpful Hints from Other Third-Grade Test Heroes!

Third graders all over Washington have good ideas about tests. Here are some of them!

- Ask yourself, "Did I answer the question that was asked?" Carefully read the question so you can give the right answer.

- Read each answer choice before filling in an answer bubble. Sometimes, you read the first choice, and it seems right. But, when you get to the third choice, you realize that's the correct answer. If you had stopped with the first choice, you would have answered the question incorrectly. It is important to read all three choices before answering the question.

- Remember, the WASL is not trying to trick you. Do not look for trick answers. There will always be a right answer. If the answer choices do not look right, mark the question and go back to it later.

- Don't look around the room. Don't worry about how fast your friends are working, and don't worry about how well they are doing. Only worry about yourself. If you do that, you will do better on the test.

Reading

Introduction

In the Reading section of the Washington Assessment of Student Learning (WASL), you will be asked questions to test what you have learned so far in school. These questions are based on the reading skills you have been taught in school through third grade. The questions you will answer are not meant to confuse or trick you but are written so you have the best chance to show what you know.

Show What You Know® on the WASL for Grade 3, Student Workbook includes a Reading Practice Tutorial that will help you practice your test-taking skills. Following the Reading Practice Tutorial, there are two full-length Reading Assessments (Reading Assessment One—Session One and Session Two, Reading Assessment Two—Session One and Session Two). Both the Reading Practice Tutorial and the Reading Assessments have been created to model the Grade 3 Washington Assessment of Student Learning in Reading.

About the Reading WASL

On the Grade 3 Reading Assessment there are five passages: two literary passages, two informational passages, and one linked pair composed of a literary passage and an informational passage (the pair counts as one passage due to its linked content). The passages may be as short as a thirty-word poem or as long as a 600-word essay. Literary passages may be poems, stories, biographies, autobiographies, or literary essays. Informational passages may be textbook entries, informational essays, instructional tasks, charts, graphs, maps, and/or timelines. There is typically a "science-like" passage and a "social studies-like" passage. The Reading Assessment is given in two sessions, Session One and Session Two. Each session will have literary and informational selections, with a total of three selections for each session.

For the Reading Assessment, you will read stories and other selections and answer some questions. There are three different types of questions. There are multiple-choice, short-answer, and extended-response questions. You may look back at the story or selection when you are answering the questions. However, you may not use resource materials during the Reading Assessment.

Item Distribution on the WASL for Grade 3 Reading

Text Types/ Strands	No. of Reading Selections	No. of Words In Text	No. of Multiple Choice	No. of Short Answer	No. of Extended Response
Literary Comprehension	3		5	1–2	0
Analysis			5	1–2	1
Informational Comprehension	3		5	1–2	0
Analysis			5	1–2	1
Total	6	Approximately 2200	20	6	2

Scoring

On the WASL for Grade 3 Reading Assessment, each multiple-choice item is worth one point. Short-answer items have three possible scores: two points, one point, and zero points. Extended responses have five possible scores: four points, three points, two points, one point, and zero points. For the most part, a short answer asks for two pieces of evidence and an extended response asks for four pieces of evidence. Responses are scored with emphasis on communication of ideas. Sentence structure, word choice, usage, grammar, and mechanics are generally disregarded unless they substantially interfere with communication.

Typical Distribution of Score Points by Item Type

Type	Number of Items	Total Points	Percent of Total Score
Multiple-Choice	20	20	50%
Short-Answer	6	12	50%
Extended-Response	2	8	
Total	**28**	**40**	**100%**

Scoring Rules for Short-Answer Items

Scoring rules for items that assess <u>main ideas and details</u>:

A **2-point** response shows thorough comprehension of the main idea and important details. It uses ample, relevant information from text(s) to support responses.

A **1-point** response shows partial comprehension of the main idea and important details (may grasp main idea but show difficulty distinguishing between important and unimportant details; may miss part of fundamental who/what/where/when/why). It attempts to use information from text(s) to support responses; support may be limited or irrelevant.

A **0-point** response shows little or no understanding of the passage main ideas and details.

Scoring rules for items that assess <u>analysis, interpretation, and critical thinking about text</u>:

A **2-point** response analyzes appropriate information and/or makes thoughtful connections between whole texts/parts of texts. It develops thoughtful interpretations of text. It uses sufficient, relevant evidence from text(s) to support claims.

A **1-point** response analyzes limited information and/or makes superficial connections between whole texts/parts of texts. It develops conventional or simplistic interpretations of text. It attempts to use evidence from text(s) to support claims; support may be limited or irrelevant.

A **0-point** response shows little or no understanding of the passage main ideas and details.

Scoring rules for items that assess <u>summarizing and paraphrasing main ideas</u>:

A **2-point** response shows thorough comprehension of main ideas.

A **1-point** response shows partial comprehension of main ideas.

A **0-point** response shows little or no understanding of the passage main ideas and details.

Scoring Rules for Extended-Response Items

Scoring rules for items that assess <u>analysis, interpretation, and critical thinking about text</u>:

A **4-point** response meets all relevant criteria. It thoroughly analyzes appropriate information and/or makes insightful connections between whole texts/parts of texts. It develops insightful interpretations of text. It uses ample, relevant evidence from text(s) to support claims.

A **3-point** response meets most relevant criteria. It analyzes appropriate information and/or makes thoughtful connections between whole texts/parts of texts. It develops thoughtful interpretations of text. It uses sufficient, relevant evidence from text(s) to support claims.

A **2-point** response meets some relevant criteria. It analyzes limited information and/or makes superficial connections between whole texts/parts of texts. It develops conventional or simplistic interpretations of text. It attempts to use evidence from text(s) to support claims; support may be limited or irrelevant.

A **1-point** response meets few relevant criteria. It shows difficulty analyzing information and/or makes weak connections between whole texts/parts of texts. It may not develop beyond literal interpretation of text. It uses little or no evidence to support claims.

A **0-point** response shows little or no understanding of the passage main ideas and details.

Glossary

antonyms: Words that mean the opposite (e.g., *light* is an antonym of *dark*).

audience: The people who read a written piece or hear the piece being read.

author's purpose: The reason an author writes, such as to entertain, to inform, or to persuade.

author's tone: The attitude the writer takes toward an audience, a subject, or a character. Tone is conveyed through the writer's choice of words and details. Examples of tone are happy, sad, angry, gentle, etc.

cause: The reason for an action, feeling, or response.

character: A person or an animal in a story, play, or other literary work.

compare: To use examples to show how things are alike.

contrast: To use examples to show how things are different.

details: Many small parts which help to tell a story.

draw conclusion: To make a decision or form an opinion after considering the facts from the text.

effect: A result of a cause.

fact: An actual happening or truth.

fiction: A selection that is made up rather than factually true. Examples of fiction are novels and short stories.

generalize: To come to a broad idea or rule about something after considering particular facts.

genres: Categories of literary and informational works (e.g., biography, mystery, historical fiction, poem).

graphic organizer: Any illustration, chart, table, diagram, map, etc., used to help interpret information about the text.

heading: A word or group of words at the top or front of a piece of writing.

infer: To make a guess based on facts and observations.

inference: An important idea or conclusion drawn from reasoning rather than directly stated in the text.

inform: To give knowledge; to tell.

informational/expository text: Text with the purpose of telling about details, facts, and information that is true (nonfiction). Informational text is found in textbooks, encyclopedias, biographies, and newspaper articles.

literary devices: Techniques used to convey an author's message or voice (e.g. figurative language, similes, metaphors, etc.).

literary/narrative text: Text that describes actions or events, usually written as fiction. Examples are novels and short stories.

main idea: The main reason the passage was written—every passage has a main idea. Usually you can find the main idea in the topic sentence of the paragraph.

metaphor: A comparison between two unlike things in which one thing becomes another thing. An example of a metaphor is, "My bedroom is a junkyard!"

mood: The overall emotion created by the author.

nonfiction: A selection of writing that deals with real people, events, and places without changing any facts. Examples of nonfiction are an autobiography, a biography, an essay, a newspaper article, a magazine article, a personal diary, and a letter.

Glossary

opinion: What one thinks about something or somebody; an opinion is not necessarily based on facts. Feelings and experiences usually help a person form an opinion.

passage: A selection or writing that may be fiction (literary/narrative) or nonfiction (informational/expository).

persuade: To cause to do something by using reason or argument; to cause to believe something.

plot: A series of events that make up a story. Plot tells "what happens" in a story, novel, or narrative poem. The plot includes rising action (introduction of the characters and their problems), climax (the most exciting moment in the story), and resolution (the final part of the story when the characters' problems are solved and the story ends).

point of view: The position or angle from which the narrator tells the story. Stories can be told in first person: one of the characters is telling the story, using the personal pronoun "I." Another point of view is omniscient, or all-knowing: the narrator knows everything about the characters and their problems.

predict: The ability of the reader to know or expect that something is going to happen in a text before it does.

prefix: A word part with its own meaning that is added to the beginning of a word to make a new word that has a different meaning.

resource: A source of help or support.

schema: The accumulated knowledge that a person can draw from life experiences to help understand concepts, roles, emotions, and events.

sequential order: The arrangement or ordering of information, content, or ideas (e.g., a story told in chronological order describes what happened first, then second, then third, etc.).

setting: The time and place of a story or play. The setting helps to create the mood in a story, such as inside a spooky house or inside a shopping mall during the holidays.

simile: A comparison between two unlike things, using the words *like* or *as*. "Her eyes are as big as saucers" is an example of a simile.

story elements: The important parts of the story, including characters, setting, plot, problem, and solution.

suffix: A unit of meaning that is added to the end of a word to make a new word with a slightly different meaning.

summarize: To briefly retell a story by listing major idea(s).

supporting details: Statements that often follow the main idea. Supporting details give you more information about the main idea.

theme: The major idea or topic that the author reveals in a literary work. A theme is usually not stated directly in the work. Instead, the reader has to think about all the details of the work and then make an inference (an educated guess) about what they all mean.

title: A name of a book, film, play, piece of music, or other work of art.

Directions for Reading Tutorial and Assessments

Directions to the Student

Today you will take the Reading WASL Assessment. This is to find out how well you understand what you read.

You will read stories and selections and answer some questions. You may look back at the story or selection when you are answering the questions. There are three different types of questions. There are multiple-choice questions that require you to choose the best answer. There are short-answer questions for which you will write phrases or sentences on the lines provided in your booklet. There are also some extended-response questions for which you are expected to write a longer and more detailed answer in your booklet.

Sample questions have been included. These sample questions do not relate to the selections you are about to read. They have been included to show you the different types of questions you will find in the booklet and how to mark or write your answers.

There are several important things to remember:

1. Read each selection. You may look back at the reading selection as often as you want.

2. The paragraphs in the reading passages are numbered. A question about a particular paragraph will refer to the paragraph number.

3. Read each question carefully. Then choose or write the answer that you think is best.

4. When you are supposed to write your answers, write them neatly and clearly on the lines provided. Cross out or erase any part of your work you do not want to include as part of your answer.

5. For short-answer or extended-response questions, you may have more space than you need. You do not need to fill the whole space. Be sure to write complete answers.

6. When you are supposed to choose a multiple-choice answer, make sure you fill in the circle next to the answer.

7. Use only a **No. 2 pencil**, not a mechanical pencil or pen, to write or mark your answers directly in the space provided in your booklet. If you do not have a No. 2 pencil, ask your teacher to give you one.

8. The Reading WASL Sample Test is un-timed, so be sure to take your time and give your best answer for each question. If you do not know the answer to a question, go to the next question. You can come back to that question later.

9. If you finish early, you may check over your work in this Reading session **only**.

10. When you reach the word **STOP** in your booklet, do **not** go on until you are told to turn the page.

Go on ▶

Sample Questions

To help you understand how to answer the test questions, look at the sample test questions that follow. These questions do not refer to the selections you are about to read. They are included to show you what the questions in the test are like and how to mark or write your answers.

Multiple-Choice Sample Question

For this type of question you will select the answer and fill in the circle next to it.

1 According to the story, which event happens first?

● **A.** Tony sees the skunk.

○ **B.** Tony drops his flashlight.

○ **C.** Tony's foot hurts.

For this sample question, the correct answer was **A**; therefore, the circle next to **A** was filled in.

Short-Answer Sample Question

For this type of question you will write a short answer consisting of a few phrases or sentences.

2 What are two similarities between Mrs. Sparrow and Mrs. Jay? Include information from the story in your answer.

Mrs. Sparrow and Mrs. Jay both go to the bird feeder every day at 6:00. Mrs. Jay says her husband built a wonderful nest for the family and Mrs. Sparrow says her husband also built a nest for the family.

Go on ▶

Extended-Response Sample Question

For this type of question you will write a more extensive answer, offering more examples and more detail.

3   What problem does Julio face?

Julio wants to get out of going to his best friends birthday dinner because he does not like what they are having.

What are **three** steps he takes to solve this problem? Include information from the story in your answer.

Julio tells his mom about the dinner and his mom says he should go to be polite.

Julio tells his friend he will go to the dinner but that he does not like carrots and gravy.

Julio goes to the dinner and is able to be polite and avoid eating the birthday dinner with carrots and gravy.

Go on ▸

Reading Practice—Tutorial

Directions: Read the story and answer the questions.

Red Riding-Hood

1   When May was six years old, her grandma made her a red coat with a hood. She looked so pretty in it that the children all called her "Red Riding-Hood."

2   One day her mama said, "I want you to take this cake and some butter to Grandma. Remember, go straight to grandma's house, do not stop on the way, and do not talk to strangers," her mama told her.

3   Red Riding-Hood was very glad to go. She always had a good time at grandma's.

4   She put the things into her little basket and ran off.

5   When Red Riding-Hood came to the woods, she met a big wolf.

6   "Where are you going?" asked the wolf.

7   Red Riding-Hood said, "I am going to see my grandma. Mama has made her a cake and some butter."

8   "Does she live far?" asked the wolf.

9   "Yes," said Red Riding-Hood, "in the white house by the mill."

10   "I will go too, and we shall see who will get there first," said the wolf.

11   The wolf ran off and took a short way, but Red Riding-Hood stopped to pick some flowers.

12   When the wolf got to the house, he tapped on the door.

13   The grandma said, "Who is there?" The wolf made his voice as soft as he could. He said, "It is little Red Riding-Hood, Grandma."

Go on ▶

14   Then the old lady said, "Pull the string and the door will open."

15   The wolf pulled the string and the door opened.

16   He ran in and swallowed the poor old lady.

17   Then he jumped into her bed and put on her cap.

18   When Red Riding-Hood tapped on the door, the wolf called out, "Who is there?" Red Riding-Hood said, "It is your little Red Riding-Hood, Grandma."

19   Then the wolf said, "Pull the string and the door will open."

20   When she went in, she said, "Look, Grandma, see the cake and butter Mama has sent you."

21   "Thank you, dear, put them on the table and come here."

22   When Red Riding-Hood went near the bed, she said, "Oh, Grandma, how big your arms are!"

23   "The better to hug you, my dear."

24   "How big your ears are, Grandma."

25   "The better to hear you, my dear."

26   "How big your eyes are, Grandma."

27   "The better to see you, my dear."

28   "How big your teeth are, Grandma!"

29   "The better to eat you."

30   Then the cruel wolf jumped up and swallowed poor little Red Riding-Hood.

31   Just then a hunter came by. He heard Red Riding-Hood scream. The hunter ran into the house and grabbed the old wolf by his feet.

32   When he turned the wolf upside down, out jumped Little Red Riding-Hood and her grandma.

Go on ▶

1   What is the meaning of the word *tapped* in paragraph 12 of the story?

     ○ **A.** Danced

     ○ **B.** Knocked

     ○ **C.** Dug

2   Which sentence best states the main idea of the story?

     ○ **A.** Do not talk to strangers.

     ○ **B.** I am going to see my grandma.

     ○ **C.** The better to eat you.

3   What do you think Red Riding-Hood will do the next time she meets the wolf? Use information from the story to support your prediction.

_____

_____

_____

_____

_____

_____

Go on ➤

4 In your own words, write a summary of the story. Include **three** main events from the story in your summary.

_____

_____

_____

_____

_____

_____

_____

_____

_____

_____

Go on ▶

Directions: Read the story and answer the questions.

The Little Pine Tree

1   A little pine tree was in the woods.

2   It had no leaves. It had needles.

3   The little tree said, "I do not like needles. All the other trees in the woods have pretty leaves. I want leaves, too. But I will have better leaves. I want gold leaves."

4   Night came and the little tree went to sleep. A fairy came by and gave it gold leaves.

5   When the little tree woke it had leaves of gold.

6   It said, "Oh, I am so pretty! No other tree has gold leaves."

7   Night came.

8   A man came by with a bag. He saw the gold leaves. He took them all and put them into his bag.

9   The poor little tree cried, "I do not want gold leaves again. I will have glass leaves."

10   So the little tree went to sleep. The fairy came by and put the glass leaves on it.

11   The little tree woke and saw its glass leaves.

12   How pretty they looked in the sunshine! No other tree was so bright.

13   Then a wind came up. It blew and blew.

14   The glass leaves all fell from the tree and were broken.

Go on ▸

15   Again the little tree had no leaves. It was very sad and said, "I will not have gold leaves, and I will not have glass leaves. I want green leaves. I want to be like the other trees."

16   And the little tree went to sleep. When it woke, it was like other trees. It had green leaves.

17   A goat came by. He saw the green leaves on the little tree. The goat was hungry and he ate all the leaves.

18   Then the little tree said, "I do not want any leaves. I will not have green leaves, nor glass leaves, nor gold leaves. I like my needles best."

19   And the little tree went to sleep. The fairy gave it what it wanted.

20   When it woke, it had its needles again. Then the little pine tree was happy.

Go on ▶

5 According to the story, which event happens first?

    ● **A.** The little tree asks for gold leaves.

    ○ **B.** The glass leaves fall from the tree.

    ○ **C.** The goat eats all the leaves.

6 According to the story, how does the little pine tree feel about the other trees in the woods?

    ○ **A.** The little pine tree is mad at the other trees.

    ● **B.** The little pine tree is jealous of the other trees.

    ○ **C.** The little pine tree is happy for the other trees.

Go on ▸

7   What problem does the little pine tree face? What are **three** steps the little pine tree takes to solve this problem? Include information from the story in your answer.

glass leavs

green leavs

gold leavs

8   According to the story, what happened when the wind blew and blew?

○ **A.** A man came by and put the gold leaves in his bag.

○ **B.** A goat ate all the leaves.

● **C.** The glass leaves fell from the tree and were broken.

Go on ➤

Directions: Read the selection and answer the questions.

A Sign of Pride

1   An important sign of the United States is our flag. Our flag stands for the land. It stands for the people. It stands for the government.

2   On June 14, 1777, the Continental Congress decided on a flag for the United States that would have 13 stripes. The stripes would be red and white. The first stripe would be red. The next stripe would be white. The stripe after that would be red, and so on. The Continental Congress also said the flag would have a group of 13 white stars on a blue background. The 13 stripes stood for the first 13 colonies. These 13 colonies were the first states in the United States. The 13 stars stood for the number of states in the United States at that time.

3   The Continental Congress did not say how the stars should be arranged. On some flags, 12 stars were placed in a circle with one star in the middle. On others, the 13 stars were placed in a circle.

4   As new states became part of the United States, more stars and stripes were added to the flag. People soon thought the flag had too many stripes. The Flag Act of 1818 stated that the American flag would only have 13 stripes, one stripe for each of the first 13 colonies. The Flag Act also said the American flag should have one white star for each state in the United States. In 1846, the flag had 28 stars. By 1861, the number of stars was 34. In 1898, the flag had 45 stars. The last change to the flag was in 1960. A star was added for the state of Hawaii. The flag with 50 stars is the one we use today.

5   The American flag has had several nicknames. Our country's earliest flag was known as the Continental flag, or the Congress colors. Today, it is called the Stars and Stripes. It is also called Old Glory or the Red, White, and Blue. No matter what name is used, the flag we see flying today is an important sign of pride for our country.

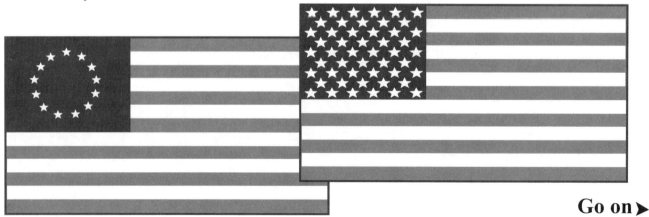

Go on ▶

9   Who would find the information in the selection most useful?

⬤ **A.** A student writing a report on flags

◯ **B.** A student writing a report on Hawaii

◯ **C.** A student writing a report on stars

10   What is the author's purpose for writing the selection?

◯ **A.** To entertain

⬤ **B.** To inform

◯ **C** To demonstrate

Go on ▶

Directions: Read the selection and answer the questions.

The Harrison Elementary Press
A Newspaper Written By Kids, For Kids

March Issue

Science Section, Page 1

FROGS AND TOADS
By Federico Garcia

1   It's important to look to see if the animal you are about to kiss is a frog or a toad. You may never find a handsome prince if you kiss the wrong amphibian. Can you tell the difference between a frog and a toad?

2   It is easy to confuse frogs and toads just by looking at them. They are both amphibians. This means they can live both in water and on land. They both are coldblooded. This means their body temperatures are the same as the air temperatures around them. They have to look for cool, shady places to rest if they become too hot. Frogs and toads look for warm, sunny places if they are too cold. Both animals are vertebrates. This means they have spines. Their body shape is almost the same. Their eyes stick out from their faces, so they can see in most directions without turning their heads.

3   Frogs and toads use their long, sticky tongues to catch insects to eat. Both frogs and toads swallow their food whole.

4   How are frogs and toads different? Frogs are better swimmers and jumpers because they have long back legs. A toad's back legs are shorter. Frogs are more likely to be found near water. Toads often live in drier places. Most frogs have four webbed feet. Toads do not have webs on their back feet. The skin of a frog is smooth and damp. Toads have drier skin that is covered with bumps called glands. Frogs have teeth in their upper jaws and no teeth in their lower jaws. Toads have no teeth at all.

5   As you can see, frogs and toads are not the same type of amphibian. Of course, a frog turning into a handsome prince only happens in fairy tales. Who would kiss a frog or a toad anyway?

Go on ▶

© Englefield & Associates, Inc.

11   Which sentence from the selection is an opinion?

　　　○ **A.** Frogs and toads are coldblooded.

　　　◉ **B.** Frogs and toads swallow their food whole.

　　　○ **C.** It is easy to confuse frogs and toads just by looking at them.

12   The author's purpose for writing the selection may have been to inform the reader about frogs and toads. Use **two** details from the selection that support this purpose.

_____

_____

_____

_____

_____

_____

Go on ➤

13 How might the selection be useful to someone who wants to get a frog for a pet? Include **two** details from the selection in your answer.

_____

_____

_____

_____

_____

_____

STOP

Reading Assessment One—Session One

Turn to page 27 to read the Directions for Session One of this Reading Assessment. Then, turn back to this page to begin.

Directions: Read the story and answer the questions.

The Farmer and His Three Sons

1   A farmer who had worked hard all his life was taken sick. He knew that he must soon die. He called his three sons about his bed to give them some advice.

2   "My sons," said he, "keep all of the land which I leave you. Do not sell any of it, for there is a treasure in the soil. I shall not tell you where to hunt for it, but if you try hard to find it, and do not give up, you will surely succeed.

3   "As soon as the harvest[1] is over, begin your search with plow, and spade, and rake. Turn every foot of earth, then turn it again and again. The treasure is there."

4   After the father died, the sons gathered in the harvest. As soon as the grain had been cared for, they planned to search for the hidden treasure. The farm was divided into three equal parts. Each son agreed to dig carefully his part.

5   Every foot of soil was turned by the plow or by the spade[2]. It was next harrowed[3] and raked, but no treasure was found. That seemed very strange.

6   "Father was an honest man and a wise man," said the youngest son. "He would never have told us to hunt for the treasure if it were not here. Do you not remember that he said, 'Turn the soil again and again'? He surely thought the treasure worth hunting for."

7   "Our land is in such good condition now that we might as well sow winter wheat," said the oldest son. His brothers agreed to this and the wheat was sown.

8   The next harvest was so great that it surprised them. No neighbor's field bore[4] so many bushels[5] of wheat to the acre. The sons were pleased with their success.

Go on ➤

9 After the wheat was harvested, they met to make plans for searching again for the hidden treasure. The second son said:

10 "I have been thinking ever since our big harvest that perhaps father knew how this search would turn out. We have much gold. We did not find it in a hole in the ground, but we found it by digging. If we had not cultivated[6] our fields well, we should not have had such a crop of wheat. Our father was wise; we have dug for the treasure and have found it.

11 "We will cultivate the ground still better next year and make the soil rich; then we shall find more treasure."

12 The other sons agreed to this. "It is good to work for what we get," they said.

13 Year after year the farm was well tilled and bore good crops. The sons became rich, and they had two things much better than wealth—good health and happiness.

---

[1] *Harvest: the gathering in of a crop*
[2] *Spade: a tool used for digging*
[3] *Harrow(ed): to break up and level plowed ground*
[4] *Bore: produced*
[5] *Bushel: a unit of dry measure for grain*
[6] *Cultivated: to have prepared soil or land for growing crops*

Go on ▶

1 According to the story, which event happens last?

    ○ **A.** The sons are pleased with their success.

    ○ **B.** The father tells the sons there is treasure in the soil.

    ◉ **C.** The sons agree it is good to work for what they get.

2 According to the story, where does the story take place?

    ○ **A.** A city

    ◉ **B.** A farm

    ○ **C.** A town

3 Which sentence explains why winter wheat was planted in the story?

    ○ **A.** Every foot of soil was turned by the plow or by the spade.

    ○ **B.** The next harvest was so great that it surprised them.

    ◉ **C.** Year after year the farm was well tilled and bore good crops.

Go on

4 Any of these titles could be another title for the story. Choose the title you think best fits the story.

Buried Treasure

The Big Harvest

Rich Soil

Use **two** details from the story to support your choice.

Buried Treasure

_____

_____

_____

_____

_____

5 What does the father mean when he says, "Do not sell any of it, for there is a treasure in the soil" in paragraph 2 of the story?

○ **A.** The treasure buried in the soil will make the sons rich.

○ **B.** The soil is the treasure that will make the sons rich.

○ **C.** The harvest the soil will provide is the treasure that will make the sons rich.

Go on ▶

Directions: Read the selection and answer the questions.

Clouds

1   Clouds are little drops of water or ice that float together through the air. Clouds come in different shapes and sizes.

2   There are three different kinds of clouds. You can tell the kind of cloud by the way the cloud looks and where it is in the sky. Some clouds are low in the sky, some are in the middle, and some are high in the sky.

3   The highest clouds in the sky are cirrus clouds. Some people think cirrus clouds look like thin white feathers. Others call cirrus clouds "mares' tails" because they look like the long tails of horses. Because cirrus clouds are so high in the sky where the temperature is very cold, cirrus clouds are made of tiny ice crystals. Cirrus clouds move quickly across the sky at about 200 miles an hour.

4   Another kind of cloud is the cumulus cloud. These clouds look like pretty white cotton balls in the sky. Cumulus clouds float low in the sky and change shape as the air moves them. Some people like to play games to guess what shape the cumulus cloud looks like: a ship, a flower, a face, or an animal. When cumulus clouds pile on top of each other they are called nimbus clouds. Nimbus clouds turn into black storm clouds that bring thunderstorms.

5   Stratus clouds are low in the sky. They look like long, gray blanket clouds. Rain and snow may fall from stratus clouds. Stratus clouds often hide the sun and the moon.

Go on ▸

6 Who would find the information in the selection most useful?

    ○ **A.** A student writing a report on clouds

    ◉ **B.** A student writing a report on weather

    ○ **C.** A student writing a report on temperature

7 What is the meaning of the word *float* in paragraph 4 of the selection?

    ○ **A.** To go from job to job

    ○ **B.** To flood or irrigate land

    ◉ **C.** To move slowly and lightly through the air

Go on ▸

8 Any of these headings could be used for the fourth paragraph. Choose the heading that best fits the paragraph.

Cotton Balls in the Sky

Cloud Watching

Cumulus Clouds

Use **two** details from the selection to support your choice.

cotten balls in the sky

Go on ➤

9   What is the author's purpose for writing the selection?

     ○ **A.** To entertain

     ◉ **B.** To inform

     ○ **C.** To demonstrate

10   Which sentence from the selection is an opinion?

     ◉ **A.** Stratus clouds are low in the sky.

     ○ **B.** These clouds look like pretty white cotton balls in the sky.

     ○ **C.** Cumulus clouds float low in the sky and change shape as the air moves them.

Go on ➤

Directions: Read the poem and answer the questions.

The Raindrops' New Dresses

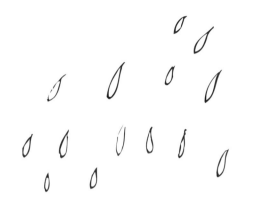

1   "We're so tired of these gray dresses!"
     Cried the little drops of rain,
     As they came down helter-skelter[1]
     From the Nimbus cloud fast train.

2   And they bobbed against each other
     In a spiteful[2] sort of way,
     Just like children when bad temper
     Gets the upper hand some day.

3   Then the Sun peeped out a minute.
     "Dears, be good and do not fight,
     I have ordered you new dresses,
     Dainty robes of purest white."

4   Ah! then all the tiny raindrops
     Hummed a merry glad refrain[3],
     And the old folks cried: "How pleasant
     Is the music of the rain!"

5   Just at even, when the children
     Had been safely tucked in bed,
     There was such a rush and bustle
     In the dark clouds overhead!

6   Then those raindrops hurried earthward,
     At the North Wind's call, you know,
     And the wee folks, in the morning,
     Laughed to see the flakes of snow.

---

[1] *Helter-skelter: with hurry and confusion*
[2] *Spiteful: having or showing a desire to cause harm or pain to others*
[3] *Refrain: a melody or tune*

Go on ▶

11 According to the poem, which event happens last?

    ○ **A.** The children went to sleep.

    ○ **B.** The Sun peeped out.

    ◉ **C.** It was raining.

12 Which sentence best summarizes the poem?

    ◉ **A.** When it is cold enough, rain turns into snow.

    ○ **B.** It snows when the children go to sleep.

    ○ **C.** Adults like to listen to the sound of the rain.

Go on ➤

13 According to the poem, describe how the raindrops feel about their gray dresses. Use **three** details from the poem to support your answer.

_____

_____

_____

_____

_____

_____

_____

_____

_____

_____

Go on ➤

14 The author of *Clouds* states, "Nimbus clouds turn into black storm clouds that bring thunderstorms." Use **two** examples from *The Raindrops' New Dresses* that show how nimbus clouds bring thunderstorms.

_____

_____

_____

_____

_____

_____

STOP

Reading Assessment One—Session Two

Turn to page 27 to read the Directions for Session Two of this Reading Assessment. Then, turn back to this page to begin.

Directions: Read the selection and answer the questions.

A Journey Through Washington

1   The Lewis and Clark Expedition[1] was one of the greatest explorations in American History. President Thomas Jefferson hired Lewis and Clark to map the way west through the new Louisiana Territory[2] to the Pacific Ocean.

2   The Expedition left its winter camp near St. Louis on May 14, 1804 and went up the Missouri River. In October, they reached the Mandan villages in what is now North Dakota. This is where they spent the winter. They headed west in the spring of 1805.

3   On October 10, 1805, they came to what is now the state of Washington. As they traveled down the Snake and Columbia Rivers, the explorers began to see signs that they were nearing the Pacific Coast.

4   On November 15, 1805, the Expedition reached "Station Camp," the place they called the "End of Our Voyage." From this camp, they took side trips along the river's north bank to Cape Disappointment. On November 24, the party decided to explore the south side of the river and set up winter camp at Fort Clatsop (near what is now Astoria, Washington).

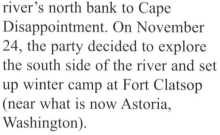

Louisiana Territory

Go on ▶

5   As soon as they thought the mountains would be passable[3] in the spring, Lewis and Clark and their party left Fort Clatsop. Following the river—first in canoes and then on land—they retraced[4] their route up the Columbia to the mouth of the Walla Walla River. Here, American Indians told them of a path to the Snake River. By following this shortcut, they saved many miles on their return journey. The route from the Columbia River to the Snake River was one of the longest by land of their trip.

6   On May 5, 1806, the Expedition left what is now the state of Washington and headed east, reaching St. Louis on September 23, 1806.

7   The Lewis and Clark Expedition completed an amazing mission. The party made many important discoveries about the native peoples of the region, the geography, wildlife, and plants of the American West.

---

[1] *Expedition: a trip made by a group of people to explore unknown territory*
[2] *Louisiana Territory: land bought by the U.S. from France in 1803; it extended from the Mississippi River to the Rocky Mountains and from the Gulf of Mexico to Canada*
[3] *Passable: capable of being crossed or traveled on*
[4] *Retraced: went back over a path or route again*

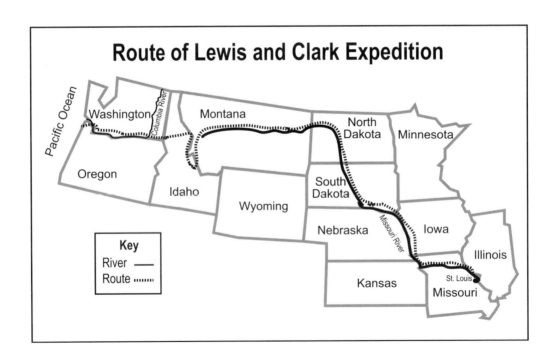

Route of Lewis and Clark Expedition

Pacific Ocean · Washington · Columbia River · Montana · North Dakota · Minnesota · Oregon · Idaho · Wyoming · South Dakota · Nebraska · Missouri River · Iowa · Illinois · Kansas · Missouri · St. Louis

Key
River ——
Route ·······

Go on ➤

15　What is the meaning of the word *route* in paragraph 5 of the selection?

　　○ **A.** A path or road for traveling from one place to another

　　○ **B.** To uncover something, especially after a search

　　○ **C.** To search for something by poking around or digging

16　According to the selection, what happened when the mountains became passable in the spring?

　　○ **A.** The Expedition set up winter camp.

　　○ **B.** The Expedition left Fort Clatsop.

　　○ **C.** The Expedition reached the Mandan villages.

17　In your own words, write a summary of the selection. Include **three** important ideas from the selection in your summary.

_____

_____

_____

_____

_____

Go on ➤

18   Who would find the information in the selection most useful?

   ○ **A.** A family planning a trip to Washington State

   ○ **B.** An author writing a story about rafting on the Columbia River

   ○ **C.** A teacher presenting a lesson on American history of the 1800s

19   The author's purpose for writing the selection may have been to inform about the Lewis and Clark Expedition. Use **four** details from the selection that support this purpose.

_____

_____

_____

_____

_____

_____

_____

_____

_____

_____

Go on ➤

Directions: Read the story and answer the questions.

The Key
by Andrea Karch Balas

1   Emma noticed a small, white box on the stairs. She picked it up carefully and opened it to find a small key wrapped in a lace handkerchief. Faded pink and blue flowers decorated the delicate handkerchief, and the initials "A.B." were stitched into one corner. Emma thought that it could belong to her grandmother because her name, Abby Brown, matched the initials.

2   As Emma examined the key, she saw that it was a dull, golden color. It was about as long as her index finger and seemed heavy for its size. There was a bit of crumpled blue ribbon looped through the hole at the top of the key. Emma thought to herself that the key must be very old because it was so worn. Emma wanted to find her grandmother and ask her about the key. As she went from room to room looking for her grandmother, Emma imagined that there might be wonderful treasures somewhere for that key to unlock. Then, Emma remembered that Gramma had gone to the store. Emma's questions would have to wait until she returned.

3   Emma was sitting on the porch step when Gramma returned. She slowly removed the key from her pocket and held it up for Gramma to see. "Look what I found—is it yours?" Emma asked. A broad smile appeared on Gramma's face as she inspected the key. "I thought I had lost this," Gramma said. "This key opens a very special box I have stored in the attic." Then, Gramma took Emma's hand and said, "Come with me. I have something to show you."

4   Emma and her grandmother walked through the house to the back stairs that led up to the attic. As they climbed the steep steps to the storage place, Emma's mind raced with thoughts about that special box. She wondered what it would look like and, most importantly, what would be inside the box.

Go on➤

20 Which word best describes how Gramma felt about Emma?

○ **A.** Angry

○ **B.** Upset

○ **C.** Kind

21 Any of these phrases could identify the author's purpose for writing the story. Choose the phrase that best describes the author's purpose for writing the story.

To entertain

To describe

To inform

Use **two** details from the story to support your choice.

_____

_____

_____

_____

_____

_____

Go on ▶

22 According to the story, after Emma went from room to room looking for her grandmother, what did she do next?

○ **A.** Emma waited on the porch step for Gramma to return.

○ **B.** Emma examined the key.

○ **C.** Emma wondered what would be inside the box.

23 Which sentence best summarizes the story?

○ **A.** "Emma noticed a small, white box on the stairs."

○ **B.** "There was a bit of crumpled blue ribbon looped through the hole at the top of the key."

○ **C.** "This key opens a very special box I have stored in the attic."

24 What is the meaning of the word *examined* in paragraph 2 of the story?

○ **A.** To inspect a patient in order to determine his or her condition or health

○ **B.** To ask questions of a witness or other party to a case in a court of law

○ **C.** To inspect or study somebody or something in detail

Go on ➤

Directions: Read the story and answer the questions.

Max, the Mischievous Macaw
by Judy Cafmeyer

1   Billy knew the routine well. It happened almost every day. It was Billy's job to look for Max. Where would he find Max? What mischief had Max gotten into? Did Max destroy anything in the house? These were the questions Billy asked himself as he searched all the rooms looking for Max.

2   Macaws are well-known for enjoying puzzles, and perhaps Max saw picking the latch on his cage as a fun puzzle to solve. At first, it was easy to find Max because the macaw wasn't familiar with the new surroundings. The bird would stay near the cage, which stood in the corner of the dining room next to the kitchen. Billy usually found Max sitting on the kitchen counter with the remnants of a pretzel feast scattered around. Recently, however, Max had started exploring other areas of the house.

3   It was Max's curiosity that caused Billy's daily task to begin. He had to locate Max and hope the cleanup would be easy.

Go on ▶

25   Any of these words could describe Max in the story. Choose the word you think best describes Max in the story.

Naughty

Playful

Difficult

Use **two** details from the story to support your choice.

_____

_____

_____

_____

_____

_____

26   According to the story, after Max got out of his cage, what did he do next?

○ **A.** Eat pretzels

○ **B.** Finish a puzzle

○ **C.** Pick the latch on the cage

Go on

27   Based on the information in the story, what do you predict Billy will do with Max?

○ **A.** Billy will let Max out of his cage.

○ **B.** Billy will put Max back in his cage.

○ **C.** Billy will put Max in the kitchen.

28   What is the main idea of the story?

○ **A.** Max likes pretzels.

○ **B.** Max likes puzzles.

○ **C.** Max is curious.

STOP

Reading Assessment Two—Session One

Turn to page 27 to read the Directions for Session One of this Reading Assessment. Then, turn back to this page to begin.

Directions: Read the story and answer the questions.

Seren and the Ladybug

1   It was 9:00 a.m. on the last day of school. Seren had a big smile on her face. She walked up to the front door. She reached for the handle and stopped. Sitting on the door handle was a small red bug with black spots. It was the prettiest bug Seren had seen. She held up her hand to the door. The bug crawled onto her finger.

2   Seren opened the door. She walked to her third-grade classroom for the last time.

3   Seren's friends were so happy about the last-day-of-school party. They could hardly sit still. They all yelled, "Hi!" and waved at Seren when she came into the room. Seren waved back with her free hand. She set her bag down on her chair and walked up to Ms. Rolson's desk.

4   "Good morning, Seren," Ms. Rolson said with a smile. She saw the small red bug on Seren's hand. "That's a very pretty ladybug you have."

5   "Ms. Rolson," Seren asked, "Is this really a bug? It looks like a bug. But it's so much prettier than all the other bugs I have seen. It's hard to believe that it's the same."

6   Ms. Rolson reached out her hand to Seren's. The ladybug crawled to the teacher's hand. "Yes, Seren, it is a bug. A ladybug is a type of beetle." Ms. Rolson held up her hand so that Seren could see the bug more closely. "See these hard, shiny parts with the spots on them?" Seren nodded. "All beetles have these. They're a type of wings. Instead of being used for flying, they're used to protect what's under them."

Go on ▶

7   "What's under them that would need to be protected?" Seren was becoming more curious about her bug.

8   "Most of the time, it's another set of wings. Many types of beetles can fly, but not as well as other kinds of bugs, such as flies. They also protect the beetles' mid-sections." At that moment, the ladybug opened its outer wings. It flew away with the softer wings hidden below. Seren jumped backward in surprise. Then, she began to laugh.

9   "Wow, Ms. Rolson. I never thought I would learn so much on the last day of school!"

Go on ▶

1   What is the main idea of the story?

○ **A.** Seren was excited about ending school for the year.

○ **B.** Seren learned about a creature she found on her last day of school.

○ **C.** Seren was working on a report about ladybugs on her last day of school.

2   According to the story, which event happens first?

○ **A.** Seren saw a ladybug on a door handle.

○ **B.** A ladybug crawled onto Seren's finger.

○ **C.** A ladybug flew away from Seren.

3   Any of these words could describe Seren in the story. Choose the word you think best describes Seren in the story.

Curious

Caring

Friendly

Use **two** details from the story to support your answer.

_____

_____

_____

_____

_____

_____

Go on

4　Which sentence explains why ladybugs have hard wings?

　　○ **A.** A ladybug is a type of beetle.

　　○ **B.** Instead of being used for flying, they're used to protect what's under them.

　　○ **C.** Many types of beetles can fly, but not as well as other kinds of bugs, such as flies.

5　What is the author's purpose for writing the story?

　　○ **A.** To persuade

　　○ **B.** To demonstrate

　　○ **C.** To inform

Go on ➤

Directions: Read the selection and answer the questions.

The Hidden Message

1　　Secret messages aren't just for detectives and spies. Some of them, the kinds that use words in place of other words or put letters in a different order, can be very hard. These are the types of secret messages that kings and rulers used when messages had to be carried on foot or by horse. If an enemy caught a soldier carrying one of these secret messages, the person sending the message hoped that the enemy would not be able to read it.

2　　Because the messages sent out by kings and rulers were usually very important, the people who were writing the secret codes wanted to make them hard to read. Not all secret codes have to be so hard, though. There are some ways that you can make simple secret messages to send to your friends.

3　　One way you can send secret messages is to use invisible ink. Invisible ink can be made in a few different ways. One way is to use lemon juice to write on a piece of paper. You can write by dipping a toothpick or the tip of a dried-out pen into the lemon juice, then use it to write as you would normally. Let the juice dry completely and give the secret message to a friend. The friend will need a parent or another adult to help read the message. Have the parent or adult hold the message up close to a light bulb, or have them hold a hot iron an inch or two above the paper. When the paper gets hot, the lemon juice will darken and the message will appear.

4　　There is another way to write an invisible message using only art supplies. Write on a piece of white paper with a white crayon. It may be difficult to see what you are writing, but when you're done, it will look like nothing is there. Anyone who wants to read the message can use water-based paint to paint over the side with the writing on it. The secret message will appear.

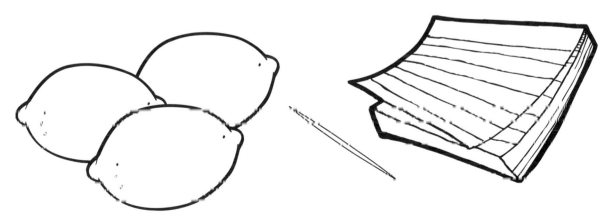

Go on ▶

6 What is the meaning of the word *invisible* in paragraph 3 of the selection?

    ○ **A.** Cannot be seen

    ○ **B.** Able to be seen

    ○ **C.** Not in the sea

7 Which sentence explains why secret messages were used by kings and rulers?

    ○ **A.** "Secret messages aren't just for detectives and spies."

    ○ **B.** "If an enemy caught a soldier carrying one of these secret messages, the person sending the message hoped that the enemy would not be able to read it."

    ○ **C.** "Anyone who wants to read the message can use water-based paint to paint over the side with the writing on it."

8 According to the selection, what happens when paper with lemon juice on it is heated?

    ○ **A.** The lemon juice will disappear.

    ○ **B.** The lemon juice will create a hole in the paper.

    ○ **C.** The lemon juice will darken.

Go on ▶

9 According to the selection, which idea does the author of the selection discuss last?

  ○ **A.** One way to send secret messages is to use invisible ink.

  ○ **B.** One way to send secret messages is to use art supplies.

  ○ **C.** One way to send secret messages is to put words in a different order.

10 How might the selection be useful to someone who wants to learn about becoming a spy? Include **two** details from the selection in your answer.

_____

_____

_____

_____

_____

_____

Go on ▸

Directions: Read the selection and answer the questions.

Bill Gates

1   Bill Gates had a dream that changed the world. Born in Seattle, Washington, on October 28, 1955, Bill Gates grew up with his parents and his two sisters. As a teenager, Bill believed that computers would change everyone's life, and he wanted to be a part of it.

2   Bill Gates went to Lakeside School in Seattle. He was very smart and got straight As in school. After school and on weekends, he worked on what he loved best: computers. Sometimes he would forget to sleep and would work all night on the computer. He knew more about computers than most grown-ups.

3   When he was 13, Bill began writing computer programs[1] that told the computer what to do. Bill knew that computers could be used for things like helping kids with math problems, writing stories, drawing pictures, or playing games.

4   In 1973, Bill went to Harvard University as a freshman. In college, Bill began to write a computer language[2]. In 1975, Bill and his old school friend Paul Allen began a company called Microsoft. Bill believed that computers would one day be used by people at work, in schools, and in homes. He knew that people would use computers to help them do their work and to have fun.

5   Bill worked for six weeks with his friend Paul to write the first computer language program. Sometimes Bill would work sixteen to eighteen hours a day to get his work done. He found his old high school and college friends to help him in his company. Sometimes they brought sleeping bags to the office so they could work long hours to finish a job. Bill still works seventy to eighty hours a week at his job.

Go on ▶

6   Bill Gates is one of the richest men in the world. He and his wife Melinda like to spend their money in ways that will help the world. They give billions of dollars to help improve[3] the learning and health of people all over the world. He even received an honorary knighthood from the Queen of England for his caring work.

7   Bill is a father of three children. When he is not working hard at his company, he likes to read or play golf.

---

[1] *Computer program: a list of instructions that tells a computer how to do a job*
[2] *Computer language: a vocabulary and set of rules for writing computer programs*
[3] *Improve: to make something better*

Go on ▶

11 The author's purpose for writing the selection may have been to inform about Bill Gates. Use **four** details from the selection that support this purpose.

_____

_____

_____

_____

_____

_____

_____

_____

_____

_____

Go on ▶

12 How might the selection be useful to someone who wants to follow a dream? Include **two** details from the selection in your answer.

_____

_____

_____

_____

_____

_____

13 Which sentence explains why Bill Gates founded Microsoft?

○ **A.** As a teenager, Bill believed that computers would change everyone's life, and he wanted to be a part of it.

○ **B.** After school and on weekends, he worked on what he loved best: computers.

○ **C.** He knew more about computers than most grown-ups.

14 What is the main idea of the selection?

○ **A.** Bill Gates is one of the richest men on Earth.

○ **B.** Bill Gates works long and hard at Microsoft.

○ **C.** Bill Gates' work has had a great effect on our world.

Go on ▶

15 According to the selection, which idea does the author of the selection discuss last?

    ○ **A.** Bill Gates wrote computer programs when he was 13.

    ○ **B.** Bill Gates works 70 to 80 hours a week at Microsoft.

    ○ **C.** Bill Gates worked 16 to 18 hours a day to start Microsoft.

16 What is the meaning of the word *improve* in paragraph 6 of the selection?

    ○ **A.** To make something stay the same

    ○ **B.** To make something worse

    ○ **C.** To make something better

17 Who would find the information in the selection most useful?

    ○ **A.** A student researching a report on computer pioneers

    ○ **B.** A student researching a report on computer languages

    ○ **C.** A student researching a report on computer brands

STOP

Reading Assessment Two—Session Two

Turn to page 27 to read the Directions for Session Two of this Reading Assessment. Then, turn back to this page to begin.

Directions: Read the story and answer the questions.

Good Morning, Sunshine

1   Annie woke up to a ray of sunlight on her face. She blinked her eyes and stretched her arms out from beneath her blankets. She couldn't believe it was morning already. It seemed as if she had just gone to sleep. Staring at the ceiling, she thought about her day and remembered what was going to happen in just two hours. Annie's stomach began to churn[1]. She sat up but fell back on her pillow. She closed her eyes again, secretly wishing it would all be over.

2   Her mother knocked and opened the bedroom door just a crack. She saw that Annie was awake. "Good morning, Sunshine. It's time to get up! You don't want to waste a second this morning."

3   But that's exactly what Annie wanted to do. Slowly, Annie pulled herself out of bed and looked around the room that was now hers. It was still a mess. Moving boxes were everywhere. Four white, empty walls stared back at her. Maybe it would be better when things were unpacked and put away. That's what her mom and dad kept telling her. Annie couldn't believe it would ever feel as comfortable as her old room.

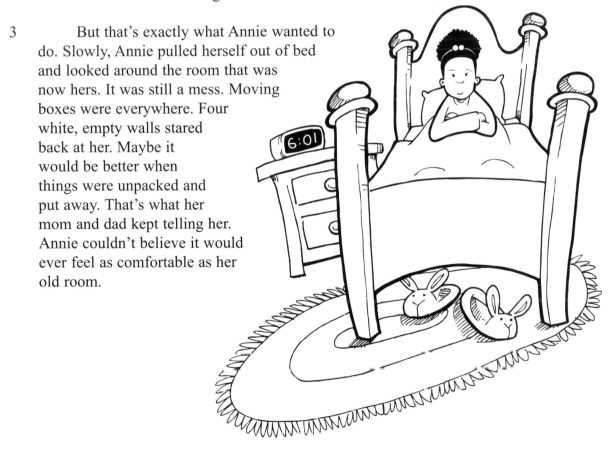

Go on ▸

4   The sunlight made it possible to study each wall. It had been too dark the night before. One wall had a tiny crack. It looked a little like a spider. "I'll never like a room with a spider crack," she thought to herself. Her mind was made up.

5   A pair of jeans, a purple shirt, and some shoes—all new—were piled in the corner. Annie's mother had surprised her daughter with the gifts yesterday. Annie knew her mother was trying to make her feel better, but Annie thought she might be more comfortable in her old clothes. New clothes never felt as good as her old ones. Annie didn't even know where to start looking for her old favorites. She settled for the new stuff.

6   "Annie, I don't hear you moving. Are you up, Sunshine?"

7   "Why does she always call me that?" wondered Annie. It was a nickname Annie didn't like, but she had grown used to it. "She should call me Grumpy," Annie whispered to herself. "That's how I feel." She tied her shoes and combed her hair. Then, she walked into the hallway and down the stairs to greet a plate of pancakes.

8   "Oh Annie, you look great!" her mom smiled as she poured a tall glass of milk.

9   "Thanks," Annie said, but she didn't mean it. Around and around, she pushed her pancakes in circles on her plate. "How can I eat?" she thought. "My insides are tied in knots." Annie watched the clock count down the remaining moments of summer.

10   "Let's go, Annie," her dad said. "You're going to miss the bus."

----

[1] *Churn: to move or stir with great force.*

Go on ▶

18   Any of these words could describe Annie in the story. Choose the word you think best describes Annie in the story.

Angry

Scared

Sad

Use **two** details from the story to support your choice.

_____

_____

_____

_____

_____

19   Based on the information in the story, what do you think Annie will do now that she is starting school in a new city?

○ **A.** She will fight with her parents and not go to school.

○ **B.** She will be nervous about meeting new people and fitting in.

○ **C.** She will be very excited to be in a new building and meet new people.

Go on ▸

20   What is the meaning of the word *unpacked* in paragraph 3 of the story?

    ○ **A.** No longer packed

    ○ **B.** Partly packed

    ○ **C.** Not yet packed

21   What is the main idea of the story?

    ○ **A.** Annie is happy and excited to be in a new house and starting classes at a new school.

    ○ **B.** Annie is mean and nasty to her parents because they moved her to a new house and a new school.

    ○ **C.** Annie is scared and nervous to be in a new house and starting classes at a new school.

Go on ▶

22 What do you think would be the best part of moving to a new place? Include information from the story in your answer.

_____

_____

_____

_____

_____

What do you think would be the worst part of moving to a new place? Include information from the story in your answer.

_____

_____

_____

_____

_____

Go on ›

Directions: Read the selection and answer the questions.

The Space Age

1   The Seattle World's Fair of 1962 was a peek into the 21st century[1]. It was the first world's fair to be held in the United States in over 20 years. The theme of the fair was "Century 21"; the focus of the fair was on space, the future, and science. Could you imagine seeing the Space Needle for the first time? Or one of the first home computers? Or the Monorail? These are all things that by the year 2000 seem "old fashioned."

2   The Seattle World's Fair was also known as The Century 21 Exposition[2]. The fair was about leaping into the future and seeing what new ideas lie ahead. The Fair was one of the most successful world's fairs in history.

3   The Space Needle was one of the symbols of the 1962 fair and is the most well known. At 600 feet high, the Space Needle has three elevators to carry passengers up to the Observation Deck, where you can see a bird's-eye view of Seattle. During the Seattle World's Fair, the Space Needle welcomed 2.3 million visitors.

4   The Space Needle was the tallest building west of the Mississippi at the time it was built. The building itself looks a flying saucer. It was one of the few buildings left standing after the fair ended.

5   The fair had many exhibitors. Exhibitors are people and companies that come to the fair and show new inventions. Some of these exhibitors presented new things like home computers. Home computers may be very common today, but in 1962 no one could believe that these machines would be so important to our future.

Go on ➤

6   There were over 29 different countries that had displays at the fair. It was wonderful to see all of these different nations represented all in the same place. They brought with them the newest and best inventions to present to the world.

7   The second most popular item at the World's Fair was the Monorail. In 1962, the price to ride the Monorail at the fair was 50 cents one-way, 75 cents round-trip for adults, and 35 cents one-way, 50 cents round-trip for children. What a deal! For just a few cents, you could ride on a high-speed monorail that was 1.2 miles long and would move people between downtown Seattle and the World's Fair site in 94 seconds.

8   The Monorail and the Space Needle were so well-known around the country that a four-cent stamp was put out with images of the Monorail and Space Needle on it.

9   Even though the fair has been gone for over 40 years, the people that went to the fair will never forget its sights and sounds. The Space Needle and the Monorail still remain as reminders of the fair of 1962. The exhibitors are now gone, but what they brought to the fair is still in many of the visitors' memories. It was a time when "the Space Age" seemed ages away.

---

[1] *Century: a period of 100 years, beginning with a year ending in 00 and runs through 99*
[2] *Exposition: a large public show*

Go on ▶

23   What does the author mean when he says "...where you can see a bird's-eye view of Seattle" in paragraph 3 of the selection?

○ **A.** A fuzzy view from high in the air

○ **B.** A clear view from ground level

○ **C.** A clear view of Seattle from high in the air

25   Which sentence best summarizes this selection?

○ **A.** The Seattle World's Fair displayed visions of future scientific discoveries.

○ **B.** The Seattle World's Fair was held so the Space Needle could be built.

○ **C.** The Seattle World's Fair introduced the world to the Monorail.

Go on ➤

24 The author's purpose for writing the selection may have been to inform about the Seattle World's Fair. Use **four** details from the selection that support this purpose.

_____

_____

_____

_____

_____

_____

_____

_____

_____

_____

_____

_____

Go on ➤

Seattle World's Fair 1962

1   The fair ran from April 21, 1962 to October 21, 1962. Attendance at the fair was 9,639,969 people. There were five main theme areas or "Worlds" at the fair. They were the World of Art, World of Century 21, World of Commerce, World of Entertainment, and World of Science. Symbols of the Fair included Man in Space and the Space Needle.

2   Some of the most popular activities at the Fair was people watching, riding the Monorail, and exploring the Space Needle. The Space Needle was built to withstand winds of up to 200 miles per hour. The elevators on the Space Needle travel at 10 miles per hour.

3   The high-speed Monorail was 1.2 miles long. More than 15,000 tons of steel were used in the construction of the Monorail. It traveled from downtown Seattle to the World's Fair in less than two minutes.

Go on ▶

26   What word could the author have used in paragraph 3 instead of *construction*?

○ **A.** Building

○ **B.** Structure

○ **C.** Materials

27   Based on information in the selection, what would happen if a severe storm with winds of 150 mph hit Seattle?

○ **A.** The Space Needle would be destroyed.

○ **B.** The Space Needle would withstand the storm.

○ **C.** The elevators on the Space Needle would stop.

Go on ▶

28　The author of The Space Age states "The theme of the fair was 'Century 21'; the focus of the fair was on space, the future, and science." Use **two** examples from Seattle World's Fair that show how Space was a theme of the fair.

_____

_____

_____

_____

_____

_____

STOP

Mathematics

Introduction

In the Mathematics section of the Washington Assessment of Student Learning (WASL), you will be asked questions to test what you have learned so far in school. These questions are based on the mathematics skills you have been taught in school through third grade. The questions you will answer are not meant to confuse or trick you but are written so you have the best chance to show what you know.

Show What You Know® on the WASL for Grade 3, Student Workbook includes a Mathematics Practice Tutorial that will help you practice your test-taking skills. Following the Mathematics Practice Tutorial is a full-length Mathematics Assessment (Session One, Session Two, and Session Three). Both the Mathematics Practice Tutorial and the Mathematics Assessment have been created to model the Grade 3 Washington Assessment of Student Learning in Mathematics.

About the Mathematics WASL

The Grade 3 Mathematics Assessment will test Content (number sense, measurement, geometric sense, probability and statistics, and algebraic sense) as well as Process (solves problems and reasons logically, communicates understanding, and makes connections). The Mathematics Assessment is given in three sessions: Session One, Session Two, and Session Three.

For the Mathematics Assessment, there are three different types of questions: multiple choice, enhanced multiple choice, and short answer. For Session One and Session Two, you will be allowed to use calculators, rulers, pattern blocks, base ten blocks, geoboards, tiles, and any other classroom tools. Dictionaries, thesauruses, and scratch paper are not allowed on any session of the Mathematics test.

Item Distribution on the WASL for Grade 3 Mathematics

Essential Academic Learning Requirement	Strand	Multiple-Choice Items	Short-Answer Items**	Extended-Response Items	Total Number of Points
Concepts & Procedures of Mathematics	Number Sense (4)*	3 – 5	1 – 2	0	5 – 9
	Measurement (4)*	3 – 5	1 – 2	0	5 – 9
	Geometric Sense (2)*	3 – 5	1 – 2	0	5 – 9
	Probability and Statistics (2)*	3 – 5	1 – 2	0	5 – 9
	Algebraic Sense (3)*	3 – 5	1 – 2	0	5 – 9
Solves Problems & Reasons Logically (3)*		1 – 2	2 – 3	0	5 – 8
Communicates Understanding (2)*		0	2 – 3	0	4 or 6
Makes Connections (1)*		1 – 2	1 – 2	0	3 – 6
Total Number of Items		**23**	**12**	**0**	**35**
Total Number of Points		**23**	**32****	**0**	**55**

*Numbers in parentheses represent the number of Learning Targets in each Strand as assessed in the Washington Assessment of Student Learning.
**Four of the short-answer questions will be double scored, once for a content strand and once for a process strand.

Scoring

On the WASL for Grade 3 Mathematics Assessment, each multiple-choice item is worth one point. Short-answer items and enhanced multiple-choice items have three possible scores: two points, one point, and zero points. Scoring will focus on the understanding of mathematical ideas, information, and solutions. Sentence structure, usage/grammar, spelling, capitals, punctuation, and paragraphing are generally disregarded as long as the wording of the response does not interfere with the mathematical communication.

Typical Distribution of Score Points by Item Type

Type	Number of Items	Total Possible Points	Percent of Total Score
Multiple Choice	23	23	42%
Short Answer (including Enhanced Multiple Choice)	12	32*	58%
Total	**35**	**55**	**100%**

Four of the short-answer questions will be double scored, once for a content strand and once for a process strand.

Scoring Rules for Short-Answer Items and Enhanced Multiple-Choice Items

Scoring rubric for Short-Answer items that assess <u>concepts and procedures</u> (content strands):

2-point response: The student shows understanding of the concepts, appropriate use of applicable information and procedures, and accurate results.

1-point response: The student shows partial understanding of the concepts with errors in the use of applicable information, or procedures that limit the viability of an answer.

0-point response: The student shows very little or no understanding of the concepts or procedures.

Scoring rubric for Short-Answer items that assess <u>solves problems</u> (define problems):

2-point response: The student defines a problem by identifying questions to be answered, missing or extraneous information, and/or what is known or unknown in a given situation.

1-point response: The student partially defines a problem by identifying some questions to be answered, some missing or extraneous information, or some of what is known or unknown in a given situation.

0-point response: The student shows very little or no understanding of how to define a problem.

Scoring rubric for Short-Answer items that assess <u>solves problems</u> (construct solutions):

2-point response: The student solves a problem by doing the following:
- shows understanding by selecting and using relevant information,
- uses appropriate strategies and/or procedures to construct a solution, and
- provides an answer that is a viable solution, mathematically correct, and answers the questions(s) asked.

1-point response: The student does one of the following:
- shows partial understanding of the problem and incomplete strategies or procedures
- uses appropriate strategies and/or procedures with missing or incorrect answer
- provides a correct answer with missing or incorrect work.

0-point response: The student shows very little or no understanding of how to solve a problem.

Scoring rubric for Short-Answer items that assess <u>mathematical reasoning</u> (analyze information):

2-point response: The student shows effective reasoning through an appropriate interpretation or comparison.

1-point response: The student shows flawed reasoning through an incomplete interpretation or comparison.

0-point response: The student shows very little or no evidence of reasoning through interpretation or comparison.

Scoring rubric for Short-Answer items that assess <u>communicates understanding</u>:

2-point response: The student shows understanding of how to gather, organize, and/or represent and share mathematical information for a given audience and purpose.

1-point response: The student shows some understanding of how to gather, organize, and/or represent and share mathematical information for a given audience and purpose; the response is not complete or is ineffectively presented.

0-point response: The student shows very little or no understanding of how to gather, organize, and/or represent and share mathematical information for a given audience and purpose.

Scoring rubric for Short-Answer items that assess <u>makes connections</u>:

2-point response: The student makes a mathematical connection, appropriately and accurately using concepts and/or procedures from two of the content strands, or identifies different mathematical representations that are equivalent.

1-point response: The student shows partially correct use of concepts or procedures from the content strands, or identifies some likenesses in different mathematical representations.

0-point response: The student shows very little or no use of concepts or procedures from the content strands or does not identify equivalent mathematical representations.

Glossary

addend: Any number being added.

addition: An operation joining two or more sets where the result is the whole.

analyze: To break down material into component parts so that it may be more easily understood.

angle: The distance, recorded in degrees (°), between two segments, rays, or lines that meet at a common vertex. Angles can be obtuse, acute, right, or straight.

area: The amount of two-dimensional space enclosed by a flat object is referred to as its area. The units used to measure area are always some form of square units, such as square inches or square meters. The most common abbreviation for area is A.

attribute: A characteristic or distinctive feature.

average: A measure of central tendency; generally, the word average usually implies the mean or arithmetic average, but it could also refer to the median or mode. *See mean.*

axes: Plural of axis. Perpendicular lines used as reference lines in a coordinate system or graph; traditionally, the horizontal axis (*x*-axis) represents the independent variable and the vertical axis (*y*-axis) the dependent variable.

bar graph: A graph that uses the lengths of rectangular bars to represent numbers and compare data.

chart: A method of displaying information in the form of a graph or table.

circle: A set of points in a plane that are all the same distance from the center point.
Example: A circle with center point P is shown below.

circle graph: Sometimes called a pie chart; a way of representing data that shows the fractional part or percentage of an overall set as an appropriately-sized wedge of a circle.
Example:

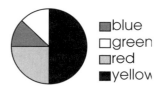

circumference: The boundary line, or perimeter, of a circle; also, the length of the perimeter of a circle.
Example:

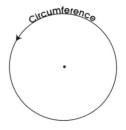

compare: Look for similarities and differences.

conclusion: A statement that follows logically from other facts.

cone: A three-dimensional figure with one circular or elliptical base and a curved surface that joins the base to a single point called the vertex.

cones

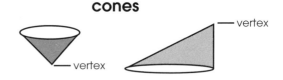

congruent figures: Figures that have the same shape and size.

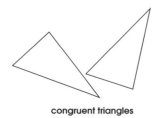

congruent triangles

cube: A rectangular prism having six congruent square faces.

Glossary

cylinder: A solid figure with two circular or elliptical bases that are congruent and parallel to each other connected by a curved lateral surface.

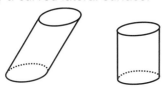

data: Collected pieces of information.

denominator: The number in a fraction below the bar; indicates the number of equivalent pieces or sets into which something is divided.

diagram: A drawing that represents a mathematical situation.

difference: The number found when subtracting one number from another; the result of a subtraction operation; the amount by which a quantity is more or less than another number.

dividend: A number which is to be divided by another number. Dividend ÷ divisor = quotient.
Example: In 15 ÷ 3 = 5, 15 is the dividend.

$$\frac{\text{quotient}}{\text{divisor}\overline{)\text{dividend}}} \qquad 3\overline{)15}^{\,5}$$

divisible: One integer is divisible by another non-zero integer if the quotient is an integer with a remainder of zero. Example: 12 is divisible by 3 because 12 ÷ 3 is an integer, namely 4.

division: An operation on two numbers to determine the number of sets or the size of the sets. Problems where the number of sets is unknown may be called measurement or repeated subtraction problems. Problems where the size of sets is unknown may be called fair sharing or partition problems.

divisor: The number by which the dividend is to be divided; also called a factor quotient.
Example: In 15 ÷ 3 = 5, 3 is the divisor.

$$\frac{\text{quotient}}{\text{divisor}\overline{)\text{dividend}}} \qquad 3\overline{)15}^{\,5}$$

edge: The line segment formed by the intersection of two faces of a three-dimensional figure; a cube has 12 edges.

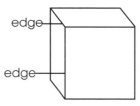

equality: Two or more sets of values that are equal.

equation: A number sentence or algebraic sentence which shows equality between two sets of values. An equation can be recognized by the presence of an equal sign (=).
Examples: 4 + 8 = 6 + 6; 4 + 8 = 24 ÷ 2; 4 + x = 12

estimate: To find an approximate value or measurement of something without exact calculation.

even number: A whole number divisible by two.
Examples: 0, 4, and 678 are even numbers.

expanded form: A number written in component parts showing the cumulative place values of each digit in the number.
Example: 546 = 500 + 40 + 6.

expression: A combination of variables, numbers, and symbols that represent a mathematical relationship.

face: A flat surface, or side, of a solid (3-D) figure. This square pyramid has four triangular faces and one square face also called its base.

factor: One of two or more numbers that are multiplied together to obtain a product, or an integer that you can divide evenly into another number.
Example: In 4 x 3 = 12, 4 and 3 are factors of 12.

figure: A geometric figure is a set of points and/or lines in 2 or 3 dimensions.

Glossary

flip: Movement of a figure or object over an imaginary line of symmetry that reverses it, producing a mirror image. Also called a reflection. Examples: Flipping a pancake from one side to the other. Reversing a "b" to a "d".
Tipping a "p" to a "b" or a "b" to a "p" as shown below:

fraction: A way of representing part of a whole set. Example:

$$\frac{\text{numerator}}{\text{denominator}} = \frac{\text{dividend}}{\text{divisor}} =$$

$$\frac{\text{\# of parts under consideration}}{\text{\# of parts in a set}}$$

function machine: Applies a function rule to a set of numbers, which determines a corresponding set of numbers.
Example: Input 9 → Rule x 7 → Output 63. If you apply the function rule "multiply by 7" to the values 5, 7, and 9, the corresponding values are:

$$5 \rightarrow 35$$
$$7 \rightarrow 49$$
$$9 \rightarrow 63$$

graph: A "picture" showing how certain facts are related to each other or how they compare to one another. Some examples of types of graphs are line graphs, pie charts, bar graphs, scatterplots, and pictographs.

grid: A pattern of regularly spaced horizontal and vertical lines on a plane that can be used to locate points and graph equations.

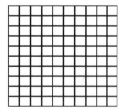

hexagon: A six-sided polygon. The total measure of the angles within a hexagon is 720°.

regular hexagon   nonregular hexagons

integer: Any number, positive or negative, that is a whole number distance away from zero on a number line, in addition to zero. Specifically, an integer is any number in the set {. . .-3,-2,-1, 0, 1, 2, 3. . .}. Examples of integers include 1, 5, 273, -2, -35, and -1,375.

intersecting lines: Lines that meet at a point.

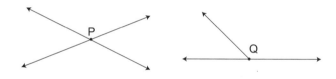

justify: To prove or show to be true or valid using logic and/or evidence.

line: One of the so-called undefined terms. As a working definition, think of it as a series of points that extend infinitely in two opposing directions.

line graph: A graph that uses lines, segments, or curves to show that something is increasing, decreasing, or staying the same over time. Note: A line graph does not have to be a straight line

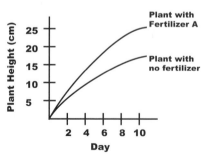

Glossary

line of symmetry: A line on which a figure can be folded into two parts that are congruent mirror images of each other, so that every point on each half corresponds exactly to its image on the other half.

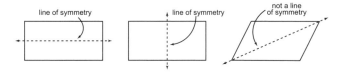

mean: Also called arithmetic average. A measure of central tendency found by adding the members of a set of data and dividing the sum by the number of members of the set.
Example: If A = 20 children, B = 29 children, and C = 26 children, the mean number of children is found by adding the three numbers (20 + 29 + 26 = 75) and then dividing the sum, 75, by the number 3. So, 25 is the mean of 20, 29, 26. The mean does not have to be a member of the set.

median: The number in the middle of a set of data arranged in order from least to greatest or from greatest to least; or the average of the two middle terms if there is an even number of terms. Example: For the data 6, 14, 23, 46, 69, 72, 94: the median is 46 (the middle number). For the data 6, 14, 23, 69, 72, 94: the median is also 46 (the average of the two middle numbers in the list). The median does not have to be a member of the set.

method: A systematic way of accomplishing a task.

mixed number: A number expressed as the sum of an integer and a proper fraction; having a whole part and a fractional part.
Example: $6\frac{2}{3}$.

mode: The item that occurs most frequently in a set of data. There may be one, more than one, or no mode. Example: The mode in {1, 3, 4, 5, 5, 7, 9} is 5. If there is a mode, it must be a member of the set.

multiple: A multiple of a number is the product of that number and an integer.
Examples: Multiples of 2 = {2, 4, 6, 8, 10, 12,....}. Multiples of 3 = {3, 6, 9, 12,....}. Multiples of 4 = {4, 8, 12,....}.

multiplication: An operation on two numbers that tells how many in all. The first number is the number of sets and the second number tells how many in each set. Problem formats can be expressed as repeated addition, an array, or a Cartesian product.

number line: A line that shows numbers ordered by magnitude from left to right or bottom to top; equal intervals are marked and usually labeled.

number sentence: An expression of a relationship between quantities as an equation or an inequality.
Examples: 7 + 7 = 8 + 6;
14 < 92; 56 + 4 > 59.

numerator: The number above the fraction bar in a fraction; indicates the number of equivalent parts being considered.

octagon: An eight-sided polygon. The total measure of the angles within an octagon is 1080°.

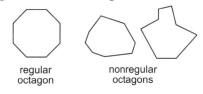

regular octagon   nonregular octagons

odd number: A whole number that is not divisible by two. Examples: The numbers 53 and 701 are odd numbers.

operation: A mathematical process that combines numbers; basic operations of arithmetic include addition, subtraction, multiplication, and division.

parallelogram: A quadrilateral with opposite sides parallel.

pattern: An arrangement of numbers, pictures, etc., in an organized and predictable way. Examples: 3, 6, 9 12 or ® 0 ® 0 ® 0.

pentagon: A five-sided polygon. The total measure of the angles within a pentagon is 540°.

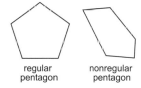

regular pentagon   nonregular pentagon

Glossary

perpendicular lines: Lines that lie on the same plane and intersect to form right angles (90 degrees).

pictograph: A graph that uses pictures or symbols to represent similar data. The value of each picture is interpreted by a "key" or "legend."

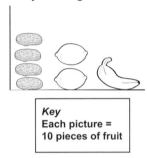

Key
Each picture =
10 pieces of fruit

place value: The value of a digit as determined by its place in a number.
Example: In the number 135, the 3 means
3 x 10 or 30. In the number 356, the 3 means
3 x 100 or 300.

point: One of the so-called undefined terms. As a working definition, think of it as a location on a graph defined by its position in relation to the *x*-axis and *y*-axis. Points are sometimes called ordered pairs and are written in this form: (*x*-coordinate, *y*-coordinate).

polygon: A closed plane figure having three or more straight sides that meet only at their endpoints. Special polygons that have equal sides and equal angles are call regular polygons.

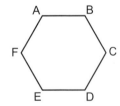

ABCDEF is a polygon.

predict: To tell about or make known in advance, especially on the basis of special knowledge or inference.

prediction: A prediction is a description of what will happen before it happens. It is a foretelling that is based on a scientific law or mathematical model.

probability: The numerical measure of the chance that a particular event will occur, depending on the possible events. The probability of an event, P(E), is always between 0 and 1, with 0 meaning that there is no chance of occurrence and 1 meaning a certainty of occurrence.

product: The result of a multiplication expression; factor x factor = product.
Example: In 3 x 4 = 12, 12 is the product.

pyramid: A solid (3-D) figure whose base is a polygon and whose other faces are triangles that meet at a common point called the vertex, which is away from the base.

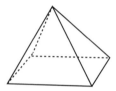

quadrilateral: A four-sided polygon. Some types of quadrilaterals have special names and properties, including rectangles, squares, parallelograms, rhombi, and trapezoids.
The total measure of the angles within a quadrilateral is 360°. Example: ABCD is a quadrilateral.

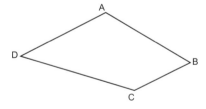

questionnaire: A set of questions for a survey.

quotient: The result of dividing one number by another number. Dividend ÷ divisor = quotient.
Example: In 15 ÷ 3 = 5, 5 is the quotient.

rectangle: A quadrilateral with four right angles. A square is one example of a rectangle.

reflection: A transformation of a figure created by flipping the figure over a line, creating a mirror image. *See flip.*

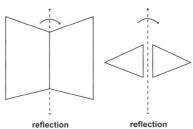

reflection   reflection

represent: To present clearly; describe; show.

rhombus: A quadrilateral with all four sides equal in length. A square is a special type of rhombus

right angle: An angle whose measure is 90 degrees. The lines or segments which form right angles are said to be perpendicular to one another. *See angle.*

right triangle: A triangle having one right angle. *See angle and triangle.*

rule: A procedure; a prescribed method; a way of describing the relationship between two sets of numbers. Example: In the following data, the rule is to add 3:

Input	Output
3	6
5	8
9	12

ruler: A straight-edged instrument used for measuring the lengths of objects. A ruler usually measures smaller units of length, such as inches or centimeters.

sample: A portion of a population or set used in statistics. Example: All boys under the age of ten constitute a sample of the population of all male children.

scale: Sequenced collinear marks, usually at regular intervals or else representing equal steps, that are used as a reference in making measurements.

sequence: A set of numbers arranged in a special order or pattern

side: A line segment connected to other segments to form the boundary of a polygon.

side

slide: Moving an object a certain distance while maintaining the size and orientation (direction) of the object. This is also known as a translation. Example: Scooting a book on a table. *See translation.*

solve: To find the solution to an equation or problem; finding the values of unknown variables that will make a true mathematical statement.

sphere: A closed surface consisting of all points in space that are the same distance from a given point (the center). Example: A basketball.

square: A rectangle with congruent sides. *See rectangle.*

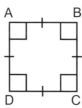

square root: The square root of a number A is the number which when multiplied by itself equals A. Example: 7 and -7 are square roots of 49 because 7 x 7 = 49 and (-7) x (-7) = 49. Every positive number has two square roots, one that is positive and one that is negative. The principal square root of a number (denoted $\sqrt{x}$) is its positive square root. Note the difference in the answers to these questions.

  1. What is the square root of 81?
     Answer: 9 and -9.
  2. What is $\sqrt{81}$?
     Answer: 9 only, not -9.

Glossary

standard units of measure: Units of measure commonly used; generally classified in the U.S. as the customary system or the metric system:

Customary System:
Length
1 foot (ft) = 12 inches (in)
1 yard (yd) = 3 feet, or 36 inches
1 mile (mi) = 1,760 yards, or 5,280 feet

Weight
16 ounces (oz) = 1 pound (lb)
2,000 pounds = 1 ton (t)

Capacity
1 pint (pt) = 2 cups (c)
1 quart (qt) = 2 pints
1 gallon (gal) = 4 quarts

Metric System:
Length
1 centimeter (cm) = 10 millimeters (mm)
1 decimeter (dm) = 10 centimeters
1 meter (m) = 100 centimeters
1 kilometer (km) = 1,000 meters

Weight
1,000 milligrams (mg) = 1 gram (g)
1,000 grams (g) = 1 kilogram (kg)

Capacity
1 liter (l) = 1,000 milliliters (ml)

---

strategy: A plan used in problem solving, such as looking for a pattern, drawing a diagram, working backward, etc.

subtraction: An operation that removes sets from an initial set, or finds the difference between two amounts when comparing two quantities.

successive events: Events that follow one another in a compound probability setting.

sum: The result of addition; addend + addend = sum.

summary: A series of statements containing evidence, facts, and/or procedures that support a result.

survey: To get an overview by gathering data.

symmetrical: Having a line, plane, or point of symmetry such that for each point on the figure, there is a corresponding point that is the transformation of that point. *See line of symmetry.*

table: A method of displaying data in rows and columns.

translation: A transformation of a figure by sliding without turning or flipping in any direction. *See slide.*

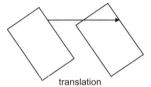

translation

triangle: The figure formed by joining three non-collinear points with straight segments. Some special types of triangles include equilateral, isosceles, and right triangles.The sum of the angles of a triangle is always equal to 180°.

turn: To move a point or figure in a circular path around a center point. Motion may be either clockwise or counterclockwise. Example: The hands of a clock turn around the center of the clock in a clockwise direction. *See rotation.*

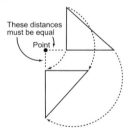

These distances must be equal
Point

undefined terms: A term whose meaning is not defined in terms of other mathematical words, but instead is accepted with an intuitive understanding of what the term represents. The words "point," "line," and "plane" are undefined terms from geometry.

whole number: An integer in the set {0, 1, 2, 3 . . .}. In other words, a whole number is any number used when counting, in addition to zero.

word forms: The expression of numbers and/or symbols in words. Examples: 546 is "five hundred forty-six." The "<" symbol means "is less than." The ">" symbol means "is greater than." The "=" symbol means "equals" or "is equal to."

Examples of Common Two-Dimensional Geometric Shapes

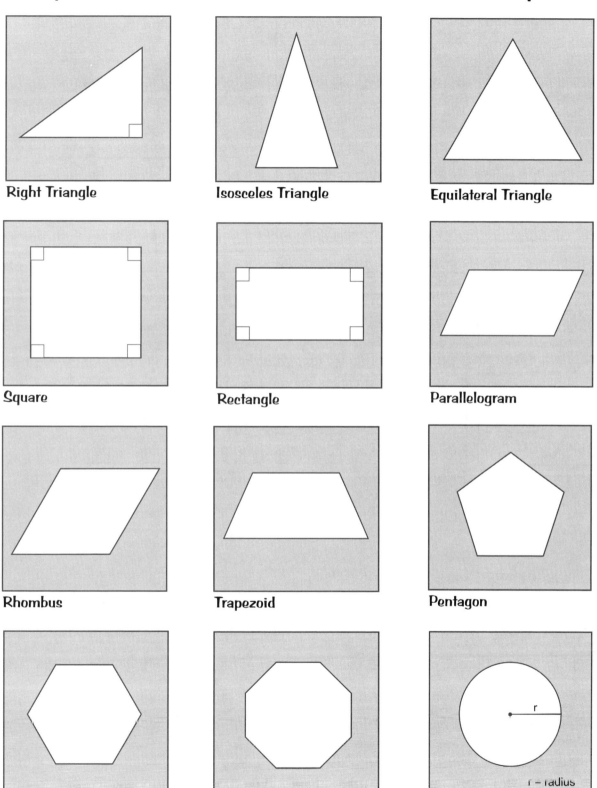

Right Triangle	Isosceles Triangle	Equilateral Triangle
Square	Rectangle	Parallelogram
Rhombus	Trapezoid	Pentagon
Hexagon	Octagon	Circle

Examples of How Lines Interact

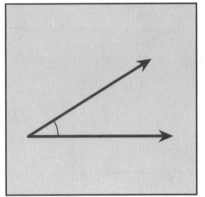

Acute Angle

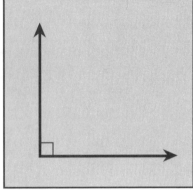

Right Angle

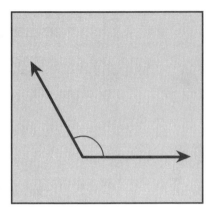

Obtuse Angle

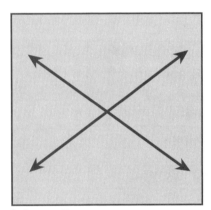

Intersecting

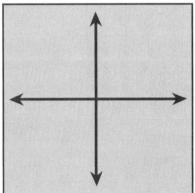

Perpendicular

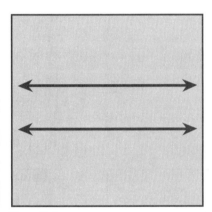

Parallel

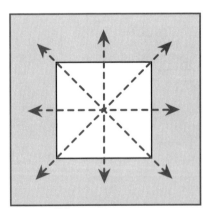

Lines of Symmetry

Examples of Common Types of Graphs

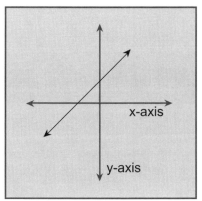

Line Graph

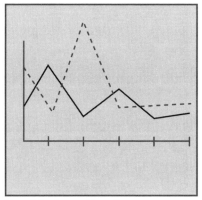

Double Line Graph

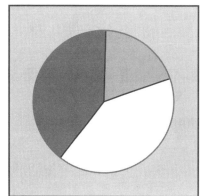

Pie Chart

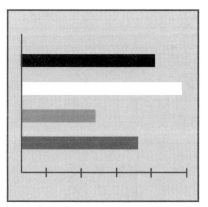

Bar Graph

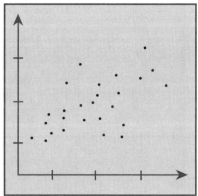

Scatterplot

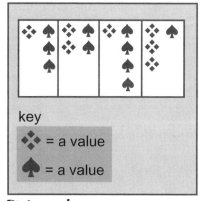

Pictograph

Examples of Object Movement

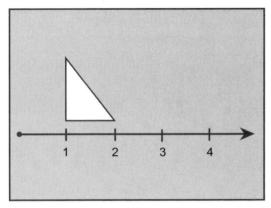 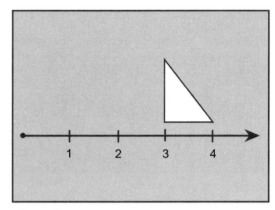

Slide (Translation)

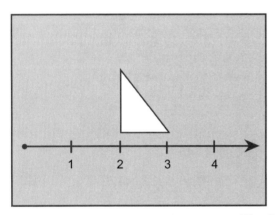 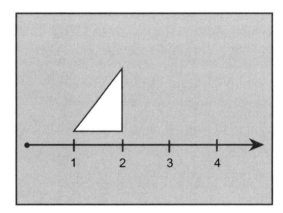

Flip (Reflection)

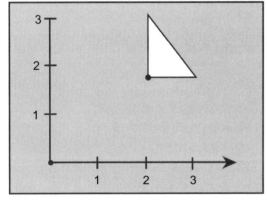 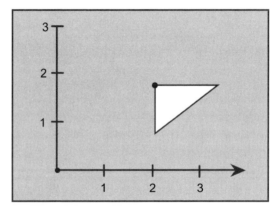

Turn (Rotation)

© Englefield & Associates, Inc.

Directions for Mathematics Tutorial and Assessment

Mathematics

Today you will take the Washington Assessment of Student Learning in Mathematics. On Session One and Session Two of the test, you are permitted to use tools such as calculators, rulers, and manipulatives. On Session Three of the test, you are **not** permitted to use tools such as calculators, rulers, and manipulatives.

Directions to the Student

There are several different types of questions on this test:

1. Some questions will ask you to choose the best answer from three answer choices. These items are worth one point.
2. Some questions will ask you to choose the best answer from three answer choices **and** then tell why you chose that answer. These items are worth two points.
3. Some questions will ask you to write your answer in an answer box.
   - Some of these questions are short. They ask you to write an answer, to explain your thinking using words, numbers, or pictures, or show the steps you used to solve a problem. These items are worth two points.

Here are some important things to remember as you take this test:

1. Read each question carefully and think about the answer.
2. If answer choices are given, choose the best answer by filling in the circle in front of your answer.
3. If an answer box is provided, write your answer neatly and clearly **inside** the box and show all your work. Cross out any work you do not want as part of your answer. **Do not use scratch paper.**
4. Use only a **No. 2 pencil**, not a mechanical pencil or pen, to write your answers directly in your test booklet. If you do not have a No. 2 pencil, ask your teacher to give you one.
5. You should have plenty of time to finish every question on the test. If you do not know the answer to a question, go on to the next question. You can come back to that question later.
6. When you reach the word **STOP** in your booklet, you have reached the end of Session One.
7. Do not look ahead to the questions in the next sessions.
8. You may check your work in Session One **only**.

Go on ➤

Sample Questions

To help you understand how to answer the test questions, look at the sample test questions that follow. They are included to show you what the questions in the test are like and how to mark or write your answers.

Multiple-Choice Sample Question

For this type of question you will select the answer and fill in the circle next to it.

1   William's basketball team is having a pizza party. There are eight players on the team. Three pizzas with eight slices each have been ordered. Each player will get an equal amount of pizza. How much pizza will each player get?

     ○ **A.** 1 slice

     ○ **B.** 6 slices

     ● **C.** 3 slices

For this sample question, the correct answer was **C**; therefore, the circle next to **C** was filled in.

Short-Answer Sample Question

For this type of question you will write an answer using words, numbers, or pictures.

2   Kathy has two packs of gum with five pieces in each pack. She wants to share the gum equally with her friends, Stephanie and Missy. How many pieces of gum will each of the girls have if they are only given whole pieces of gum? Show or explain your work using words, numbers, and/or pictures.

Each girl will have __**3**__ pieces of gum.

2 packs of gum with 5 pieces each
5 + 5 = 10 pieces of gum

    Kathy   *Stephanie*   *Missy*
    ||| *|||*   *|||*

3 + 3 + 3 + 1 piece of gum left over = 10

Go on ▶

Enhanced Multiple-Choice Sample Question

For this type of question you will select the best answer and fill in the circle next to it. Then you will tell why you chose that answer, using words, numbers, or pictures.

3 Pat had 12 seeds and 3 pots to put them into. He put the same number of seeds into each pot. How many seeds did Pat put into each pot?

● **A.** 4

○ **B.** 3

○ **C.** 6

Explain your answer using words, numbers, or pictures.

4 seeds + 4 seeds + 4 seeds = 12 seeds

1 pot + 1 pot + 1 pot = 3 pots

Go on ▶

Mathematics Practice Tutorial

1   Kim is counting the flowers in her garden. She counts 100 red flowers, 60 yellow flowers, and 2 blue flowers. She writes 100 + 60 + 2 to show the total number of flowers. How is the total written in words?

   ○ **A.** One hundred sixty-two

   ○ **B.** One hundred eighty

   ○ **C.** One thousand sixty-two

2   Which of the following is a true number sentence?

   ○ **A.** $6,987 < 6,897$

   ○ **B.** $7,968 < 6,978$

   ○ **C.** $9,876 > 9,678$

Go on ➤

3   Can you decide if this is a true number sentence without adding? Write a sentence to explain why or why not.

9 + 17 + 22 = 22 + 17 + 9

Go on ▶

4   Devon has 7 flowerpots. She wants to plant 4 flower seeds in each pot. How many seeds will she need? Show or explain your work using words, numbers, and/or pictures.

○ **A.** 21 seeds

○ **B.** 24 seeds

○ **C.** 28 seeds

Devon will need _____ seeds.

Go on ▶

5 Sasha has the coins shown below:

She buys a candy bar that costs 60¢. How much money does she have left?

○ **A.** 15¢

○ **B.** 20¢

○ **C.** 25¢

Go on ▶

6 Nick solved an addition problem. His answer is shown below:

```
   37
   42
   56
 + 28
 -----
  198
```

Estimate to the nearest 10 to check Nick's answer. Do you think his answer is correct? Write a sentence to explain why or why not.

Go on ▶

7   Trevor began watching a movie at 2:00 p.m. The movie lasted for 1 hour and 40 minutes. Which clock shows the time when the movie ended?

○ A.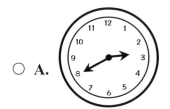

○ B.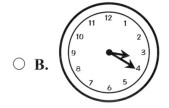

○ C.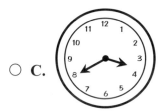

Go on▶

8 Matt used a pencil to measure the top of his desk. Matt's friend Eric used a marker to measure the top of his desk. Can they tell from their measurements if one of their desks is bigger than the other? Write a sentence to explain your answer.

Go on ▶

9 Holly needs 8 feet of ribbon for an art project. At the store they sell ribbon by the yard. How many yards does she need to buy?

    ○ **A.** 3 yards

    ○ **B.** 4 yards

    ○ **C.** 5 yards

10 Carla walked all the way around her block. What measurement will tell how far Carla walked?

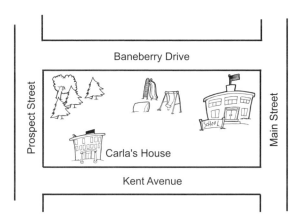

    ○ **A.** Perimeter of the block

    ○ **B.** Length of the block

    ○ **C.** Area of the block

Go on ➤

11   Mark wants to hold his breath for one minute. He wants his friend Tom to time him while he
      holds his breath, but they don't have a stopwatch. What could Tom do to estimate one minute?

    ○ **A.** Count to 6

    ◉ **B.** Count to 60

    ○ **C.** Count to 600

12   Which pair of figures is congruent?

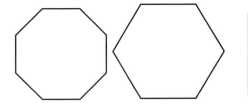  

○ **A.**

○ **B.**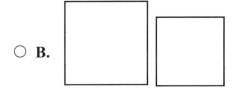

◉ **C.**

Go on ➤

13   Which of the shapes below has more angles than a square?

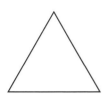  

○ **A.**

○ **B.**

● **C.**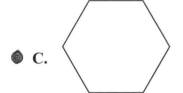

Go on ▶

14 Draw points on the number line to show these values:

53, 58, 60, 65, 74, 79

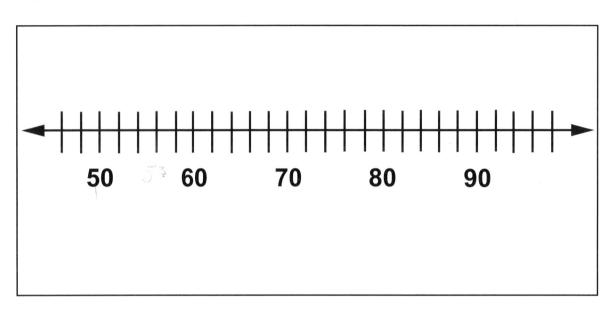

15 Luis wants to know more about his classmates and what they do when they are not at school.

Write a question Luis could ask his classmates to find out more about them.

Go on ➤

Luis asked his classmates to name their favorite after-school activity. He recorded their answers in the tally table shown below.

Use the tally table to answer questions 16 and 17.

Favorite After-School Activities

Watching TV					
Playing video games	ⅢⅡ II
Riding bikes	ⅢⅡ II
Playing with pets	II
Playing a sport	ⅢⅡ IIII

16   According to Luis' tally table, what is the mode or most common number of Luis' set of data?

⭕ **A.** 5

⭕ **B.** 9

⭕ **C.** 7

17   According to Luis' tally table, how many votes did the most popular after-school activity receive?

⭕ **A.** 7

⭕ **B.** 8

⭕ **C.** 9

Go on

18   What are the missing numbers in the pattern below?

_____ , 18, 27, _____ , 45, 54

Write a sentence to explain your answer.

_____ , 18, 27, _____ , 45, 54

19   There are 27 students in Adam's class. Eleven students are absent. Which equation should you use to find how many students are present?

    ○ A. ☐ – 27 = 11

    ○ B. 27 – 11 = ☐

    ○ C. ☐ – 11 = 27

20   Which of the expressions below shows the rule for this Function Machine?

IN	OUT
24	21
12	9
17	14
11	8
5	2
9	6

    ○ A. ☐ – 3

    ○ B. ☐ + 3

    ○ C. ☐ x 3

Go on ▶

21   Hector had $9.00. His grandmother gave him money for his birthday, and then he had $14.00 altogether. How much money did Hector's grandmother give him?

○ **A.** $3.00

○ **B.** $5.00

○ **C.** $7.00

Show or explain your work using words, numbers, and/or pictures.

Hector's grandmother gave him $ _____.

Go on ➤

22 Virginia spent $3.00 on a notebook and $1.50 on a pen. Lauren wants to know if Virgina will have enough money left to see a movie that costs $4.00.

What does Lauren need to know to figure out if Virginia can go to the movie with her?

○ **A.** The total amount of money Virginia spent on the notebook and pen.

○ **B.** The total amount of money that Virginia spent on the notebook and pen, plus the cost of the movie.

○ **C.** The total amount of money Virginia had before she bought the notebook and the pen.

Go on ▶

23 Luis asked his classmates to name their favorite after-school activity. He recorded their answers in the tally table shown below.

Favorite After-School Activities

Watching TV	IIII
Playing video games	HHT II
Riding bikes	HHT II
Playing with pets	II
Playing a sport	HHT IIII

Luis decides that his classmates spend more time playing video games than riding bikes. Do you agree? Write a sentence to explain why or why not.

Go on ▶

24   Sally is walking to her friends house that is three blocks away. Sally can walk one block in 10 minutes. What time will Sally get to her friends house?

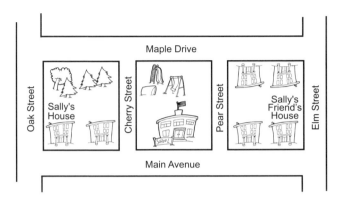

Identify the known and unknown information that should be used to solve this problem.

25   Sue has invited 12 friends to her birthday party. She wants to have 3 balloons for each of her friends.

How many balloons does she need? Show or explain your work using words, numbers, and/or pictures.

Sue needs _____ **balloons.**

Go on ▶

26 Tanya has 20 pieces of candy that she wants to divide equally among herself and 4 friends. She divides the pieces of candy into 5 piles.

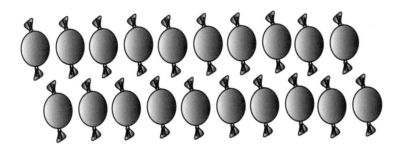

How many pieces of candy are in each pile? Show or explain your work using words, numbers, and/or pictures.

> **There are _____ pieces of candy in each pile.**

Go on ▶

27   Lindsey has $5.00. She wants to order a sandwich, drink, and ice cream from the lunch menu:

Lunch Menu

Peanut Butter and
Jelly Sandwich
$3.50

Lemonade
$1.00

Ice Cream Cone
$2.65

Does Lindsey have enough money for this lunch? Show or explain your work using words, numbers, and/or pictures.

Does Lindsey have enough money for this lunch? _____

Go on ▶

28 Mary wants to know about how much her dog Rex weighs, but she doesn't have a scale. She knows that her friend Tara's dog weighs about 40 pounds. Mary decides that Rex also weighs about 40 pounds.

Explain why this may or may not be a good estimate. Use words, numbers, and/or pictures.

Go on ➤

29 Which of the expressions below represents the rule for this number pattern?

4, 8, 12, 16, 20, 24

○ A. ☐ + 2

○ B. ☐ x 2

○ C. ☐ + 4

Go on ➤

Carly takes a survey of her class to find out what pets they have. She makes a tally mark for every pet. Use Carly's tally table to answer questions 30 and 31.

Pets

Dogs	‖‖‖ ‖‖‖ ‖
Cats	‖‖‖ ‖‖‖‖
Birds	‖‖‖
Fish	‖‖‖ ‖‖

30 According to Carly's data table, what is the total number of cats and dogs she and her classmates have? Show or explain your work using words, numbers, and/or pictures.

Carly and her classmates have _____ cats and dogs.

Go on ▸

31 Draw a bar graph to show the results of Carly's survey. Use the information in Carly's tally table on page 131.

   • Write a title for the bar graph.

   • Label and number the scale.

   • Draw the bars.

   • Label each bar.

   • Include a label for all the bars together.

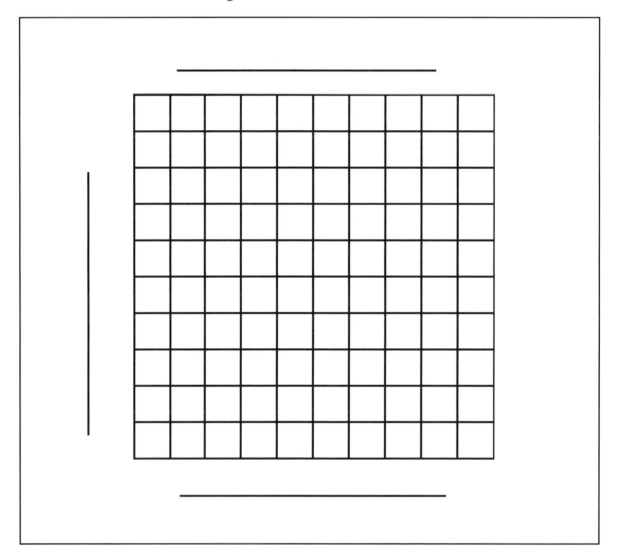

Go on ➤

32   There were 18 birds eating at a bird feeder; then some of the birds flew away. There were 7 birds left.

Write an equation to find how many birds flew away.

Go on

33　Draw a figure with the following attributes:

- Closed

- 5 sides

- 2 right angles

Go on ▶

34 Philip has $3.65. He wants to buy an ice cream cone that costs $1.50. Which group of bills and coins shows the correct change?

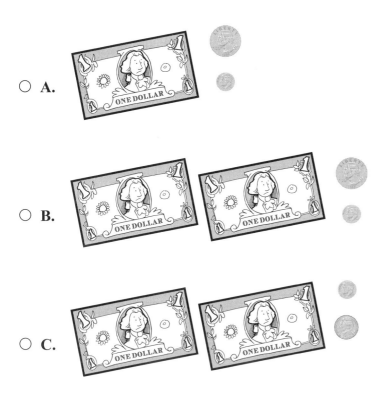

○ **A.**

○ **B.**

○ **C.**

Go on ▶

35   What number is the same as "twenty-three thousand eight hundred four"?

   ○ **A.** 2,384

   ○ **B.** 23,804

   ○ **C.** 23,840

STOP

Mathematics Assessment—Session One

On this part of the test you are permitted to use tools such as calculators, rulers, and manipulatives.

Turn to page 105 to read the Directions for Session One of this Assessment. Then turn back to this page to begin.

1   Which of these number sentences is correct?

    ○ **A.** $300 + 40 + 2 = 360$

    ○ **B.** $400 + 30 + 6 = 409$

    ○ **C.** $500 + 10 + 2 = 512$

2   Which number sentence is true?

    ○ **A.** $16 = 9 + 6 = 4 + 5 + 6$

    ○ **B.** $17 = 8 + 9 = 8 + 3 + 3$

    ○ **C.** $18 = 12 + 6 = 8 + 4 + 6$

Go on ▶

3 What is the result of adding zero to a number? Write a sentence to explain.

Go on ➤

© Englefield & Associates, Inc.

4 There are 30 students in Jay's class. Half of the class is going to the zoo on a field trip. They will see the zoo in groups of 5. How many groups of students will there be?

○ **A.** 3

○ **B.** 5

○ **C.** 10

Show or explain your work using words, numbers, and/or pictures.

> **There are** _____ **groups of students.**

Go on ➤

5 Ben and his mother baked 36 cookies. They ate 5 cookies and gave 12 cookies to a neighbor. How many cookies do they have left?

○ **A.** 17

○ **B.** 19

○ **C.** 24

Show or explain your work using words, numbers, and/or pictures.

Ben and his mother have _____ cookies left.

6   Which question could you answer without measuring?

○ **A.** Who is the tallest student in your class?

○ **B.** How tall is the tallest student in your class?

○ **C.** Which student in your class has grown the most in height since the beginning of the school year?

7   Suppose you bought a new bicycle at the store. List two measurements you can use to describe your new bicycle to a friend.

Go on ▶

8 Which statement is true about congruent figures?

○ **A.** They have the same shape, but they may be different sizes.

○ **B.** They have the same shape, and they are the same size.

○ **C.** They may have different shapes, but they are the same size.

Luis asked his classmates to name their favorite after-school activity. He recorded their answers in the tally table shown below. Use the tally table to answer questions 9 and 10.

Favorite After-School Activities

Watching TV	‖‖
Playing video games	卌 ‖
Riding bikes	卌 ‖
Playing with pets	‖
Playing a sport	卌 ‖‖

9 How many classmates did Luis ask about their favorite after-school activity?

   ○ **A.** 29

   ○ **B.** 28

   ○ **C.** 27

10 In Luis' tally table, which after-school activity received 9 votes?

   ○ **A.** Riding bikes

   ○ **B.** Playing a sport

   ○ **C.** Playing video games

Go on ▶

11 Which two shapes come next in the pattern below?

A.

B.

C.

Go on ▶

12　Valerie had 8 stamps in her stamp collection. Her uncle gave her more stamps for her birthday. Now she has 14 stamps altogether.

Which equation could you use to find how many stamps Valerie's uncle gave her for her birthday?

○ **A.** $8 + \boxed{} = 14$

○ **B.** $\boxed{} - 8 = 14$

○ **C.** $14 + 8 = \boxed{}$

Go on ▸

13 Corey is collecting shells at the beach. He finds 8 shells in the morning. By dinnertime, he has 26 shells. How many shells did he collect in the afternoon?

• Write an equation to find the answer.

• Solve the equation to find the number of shells.

Corey collected _____ shells in the afternoon.

STOP

Mathematics Assessment—Session Two

On this part of the test you are permitted to use tools such as calculators, rulers, and manipulatives.

Turn to page 105 to read the Directions for Session Two of this Assessment. Then turn back to this page to begin.

14   Why is the number 4,732 greater than the number 4,371?

○ **A.** The number in the thousands place in 4,732 is greater than the number in the thousands place in 4,371.

○ **B.** The number in the hundreds place in 4,732 is greater than the number in the hundreds place in 4,371.

○ **C.** The number in the ones place in 4,732 is greater than the number in the ones place in 4,371.

Go on ➤

15 Brad has 20 quarters. To find out how many dollars they equal, he divides the quarters into piles with 4 quarters in each pile. How many piles are there?

○ **A.** 4 piles

○ **B.** 5 piles

○ **C.** 10 piles

Go on ▸

Copying is Prohibited
© Englefield & Associates, Inc.

16   Multiplication is the same as adding equal groups. Look at the picture below:

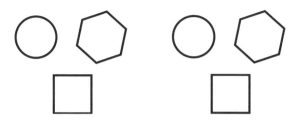

The picture shows these number sentences:

$3 + 3 = 6$

$2 \times 3 = 6$

• Write two number sentences shown by the picture below:

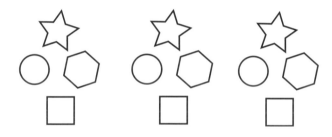

Go on ➤

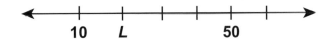

17   On the number line below, what number does *L* represent?

```
          |     |     |     |     |     |
         10    L                50
```

○ **A.** 11

○ **B.** 15

○ **C.** 20

18   Lisa went to the store to buy bananas. Bananas cost 50¢ for 1 pound. How much do the bananas on the scale cost?

○ **A.** $1.50

○ **B.** $1.75

○ **C.** $2.00

Show or explain your work using words, numbers, and/or pictures.

The bananas on the scale cost $_____

Go on ▸

19   Which unit of measure should you use to measure the weight of a car?

     ○ **A.** Ounce

     ○ **B.** Pound

     ○ **C.** Ton

20   Which drawing shows a closed shape with four straight sides, all the same length, and four right angles?

     ○ **A.**

     ○ **B.**

     ○ **C.**

Go on ▶

21   Which two figures are congruent?

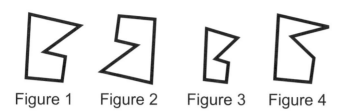

Figure 1   Figure 2   Figure 3   Figure 4

○ **A.** Figure 1 and Figure 2

○ **B.** Figure 2 and Figure 3

○ **C.** Figure 1 and Figure 4

Go on ➤

Amanda asked the workers in the school cafeteria to count the number of lunch items sold in a week. The 5 most popular lunch items are shown below in the bar graph. Use the bar graph to answer questions 22 and 23.

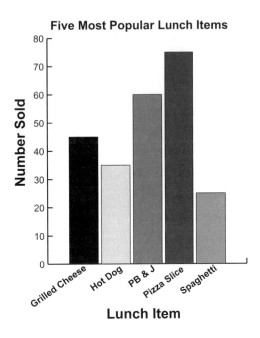

22 Which lunch item was the most popular?

◯ **A.** Spaghetti

◯ **B.** Hot dog

◯ **C.** Pizza slice

23 Which of the choices below shows the lunch items listed in order from least popular to most popular?

◯ **A.** Pizza slice, PB & J sandwich, grilled cheese sandwich, hot dog, spaghetti

◯ **B.** PB & J sandwich, pizza slice, hot dog, grilled cheese sandwich, spaghetti

◯ **C.** Spaghetti, hot dog, grilled cheese sandwich, PB & J sandwich, pizza slice

Go on ➤

24 Jamal asked his friends to name their favorite subjects in school. He made a bar graph to show the data for the five most popular subjects.

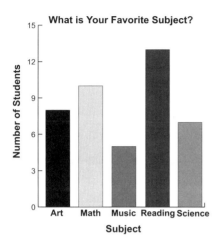

How many more students chose reading than music? Show or explain your work using words, numbers, and/or pictures.

How many more students chose reading?_____

Go on ❯

25   What two shapes come next in the pattern below?

○ A. ▢ △

○ B. △ ▢

○ C. ◯ △

Go on ▶

26 What two shapes come next in the pattern below?

○ **A.**

○ **B.**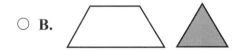

○ **C.**

Go on ➤

27 What is the missing number in this equation?

$$17 + \boxed{} = 23$$

○ **A.** 5

○ **B.** 6

○ **C.** 7

STOP

Mathematics Assessment—Session Three

On this part of the test you are **not** permitted to use tools such as calculators, rulers, and manipulatives.

Turn to page 105 to read the Directions for Session Three of this Assessment. Then turn back to this page to begin.

28   Which picture shows $18 \div 3 = 6$?

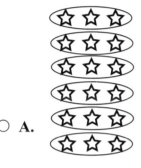

○ **A.**

○ **B.**

○ **C.**

Go on >

29 Kris has 4 rosebushes in her yard. She picks 3 roses from each bush. She wants to put the roses into 2 vases, with the same number of roses in each vase. How many roses will she put into each vase?

○ **A.** 3

○ **B.** 6

○ **C.** 12

Show or explain your work using words, numbers, and/or pictures.

Kris will put _____ roses into each vase.

Go on ➤

30 What is the total value of the coins shown below?

○ **A.** 41¢

○ **B.** 46¢

○ **C.** 51¢

31 Shauna has 78 rocks in her rock collection. During the summer, she collects 17 more rocks. Then she gives 12 rocks to one of her friends. About how many rocks does Shauna have now?

○ **A.** 90

○ **B.** 100

○ **C.** 110

Go on ▸

32 Maria wants to measure the weight of her two-year-old dalmation puppy. Which unit of measurement should she use?

   ○ **A.** Ounce

   ○ **B.** Pound

   ○ **C.** Ton

Go on ➤

33   Which diagram shows a true fact about closed figures with four sides?

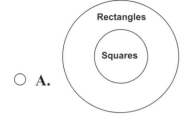

○ **A.**

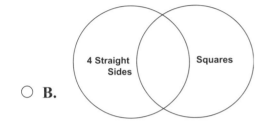

○ **B.**

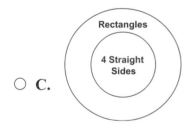

○ **C.**

• Write a sentence to explain your answer.

34   Which of the following shows all four numbers rounded to the nearest ten?

42   45   47   51

○ **A.** 40   50   50   50

○ **B.** 40   40   50   50

○ **C.** 40   40   40   50

35   On the number line below, what letter represents 45?

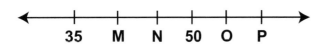

35   M   N   50   O   P

○ **A.** M

○ **B.** N

○ **C.** O

Go on ❯

Mike asked his classmates to name their favorite drinks. He made a picture graph to show their answers. Use the picture graph to answer questions 36 and 37.

Favorite Drinks
Milk
Lemonade
Water
Sports Drink
Fruit Juice

= 2 votes

36 How many votes did milk receive?

○ **A.** 3

○ **B.** 5

○ **C.** 6

37 Which drink received the fewest votes?

○ **A.** Lemonade

○ **B.** Water

○ **C.** Milk

Go on ▶

38　Write a two or three sentence story problem you can solve using the equation shown below.

　□ + 5 = 15

Go on ▶

39   Choose the best estimate for the length of a playground.

     ○   **A.**   100 centimeters

     ○   **B.**   100 meters

     ○   **C.**   100 kilometers

Go on ➤

40 Dawn had a birthday party. Her birthday cake was cut into 18 pieces. After the party, there were 6 pieces of cake left over. How many pieces of cake were served at Dawn's birthday party?

○ **A.** 9

○ **B.** 12

○ **C.** 14

Show or explain your work using words, numbers, and/or pictures.

Dawn served _____ pieces of cake at her party.

STOP

Notes

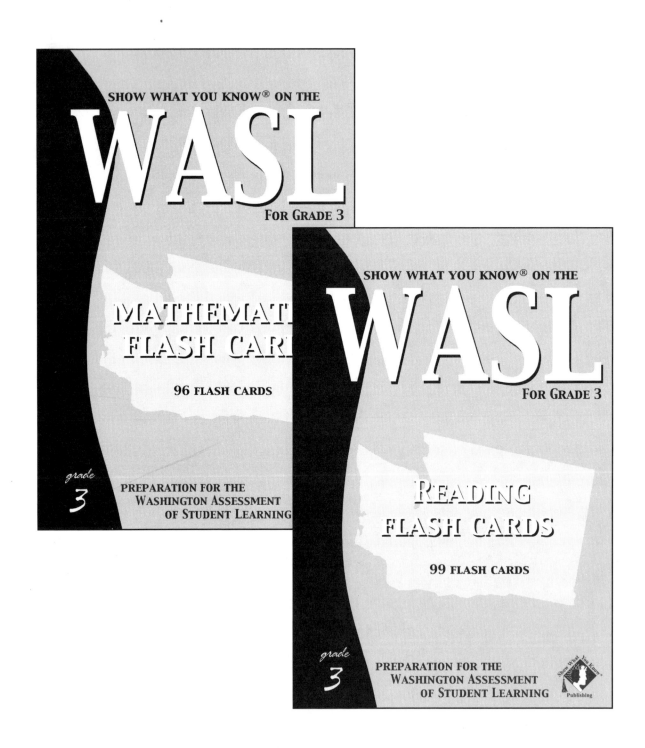